Historical Association Studies

The Cold War

Historical Association Studies

General Editors: Muriel Chamberlain, H. T. Dickinson and Joe Smith

Published Titles

China in the Twentieth Century (second edition)
Paul Bailey
* Postwar Japan: 1945 to the Present
Paul Bailey
The British Welfare State
John Brown
The Causes of the English Civil War
Norah Carlin
Decolonization: The Fall of the European Empires (second edition)
M. E. Chamberlain
From Luddism to the First Reform Bill: Reform in England 1810–1832
J. R. Dinwiddy
The Reformation in Germany
C. Scott Dixon
Radicalism in the English Revolution 1640–1660
F. D. Dow
British Politics Since 1945 (second edition)
David Dutton
The French Revolution
Alan Forrest
Britain and European Cooperation since 1945
Sean Greenwood
Oliver Cromwell
Peter Gaunt
Occupied France: Collaboration and Resistance 1940–1944
H. R. Kedward

The Vikings in Britain
Henry Loyn
Appeasement (second edition)
Keith Robbins
The Cold War (second edition)
Joe Smith
* Britain in the 1930s
Andrew Thorpe
The Normans in Britain
David Walker
Bismarck
Bruce Waller
The Russian Revolution 1917–1921
Beryl Williams
The Making of Modern South Africa (third edition)
Nigel Worden
* Lloyd George
Chris Wrigley

Forthcoming Titles

The Italian Renaissance
Peter Denley
The Whig Supremacy
H. T. Dickinson
The Enlightenment
Martin Fitzpatrick
The American Revolution
Keith Mason
The Spanish Inquisition
Helen Rawlings
The Origins of the Second World War
Glyn Stone

* out of print

The Historical Association, founded in 1906, brings together people who share an interest in, and love for, the past. It aims to further the study and teaching of history at all levels: teacher and student, amateur and professional. This is one of over 100 publications available at preferential rates to members. Membership also includes journals at generous discounts and gives access to courses, conferences, tours and regional and local activities. Full details are available from The Secretary, The Historical Association, 59a Kennington Park Road, London SE11 4JH, telephone: 020 7735 3901.

The Cold War
Second Edition,
1945–1991

Joseph Smith

BLACKWELL *Publishers*

First published 1989
Second edition published 1998
Reprinted 1998, 1999, 2000, 2001

Blackwell Publishers Ltd
108 Cowley Road
Oxford OX4 1JF
UK

Blackwell Publishers Inc.
350 Main Street
Malden, Massachusetts 02148
USA

British Library Cataloguing in Publication Data
A CIP catalogue record for this book is available from the British Library.

Library of Congress Cataloging-in-Publication Data
Smith, Joseph, 1945–
    The Cold War, 1945–1991 / Joseph Smith. — 2nd ed.
        p.   cm. — (Historical Association studies)
    Includes bibliographical references and index.
    ISBN 0–631–19138–0 (pbk.)
    1. World politics—1945– I. Title. II. Series.
D843.S546   1997
909.82—dc21   97–13828
                                                CIP

Typeset in 10 on 12pt Times by Ace Filmsetting Ltd., Frome, Somerset
Printed in Great Britain by MPG Books Ltd, Bodmin, Cornwall

This book is printed on acid-free paper.

Contents

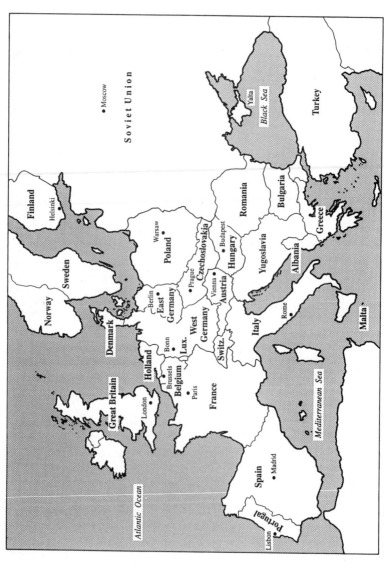

Map 1 Europe 1945 – 1990

Map 2 Asia 1950 – 1975

Preface

The first edition of this short study of the Cold War was published in 1989 and covered the years from 1945 to 1965. The close of World War II still remains a convenient point to begin a new edition. To end in 1965, however, gives a truncated and incomplete picture of the Cold War, which is now generally seen as stretching to a conclusion in 1991. I have, therefore, extended the original work to include two new chapters on *détente* and the end of the Cold War. To aid teachers and students I have also added an outline chronology, a guide to further reading and a list of abbreviations.

Joseph Smith
University of Exeter

Outline Chronology

1939	September	Germany invades Poland and begins World War II
1941	June	Germany invades Soviet Union
	December	Japan attacks Pearl Harbor, United States enters World War II
1943	November	Big Three meet at Tehran conference
1945	February	Big Three meet at Yalta conference
	April	Death of Roosevelt; Truman becomes US president
	May	Surrender of Germany marks end of World War II in Europe; Four-power control over Germany is established
	June	San Francisco Conference approves United Nations Charter
	July/August	Big Three meet at Potsdam conference
	September	Surrender of Japan marks end of war in Far East; Ho Chi Minh declares independence of Vietnam
1946	February	Kennan sends 'Long Telegram' from Moscow
	March	United States criticizes Soviet occupation of northern Iran
	December	First Indochina War begins between France and Vietminh
1947	March	Truman Doctrine announced to aid Greece and Turkey
	June	Marshall Plan announced to promote European

		economic recovery
	July	Article by Kennan publicizes the term 'containment'
	September	Rio Treaty signed to defend the western hemisphere
	October	Soviet Union establishes the Cominform
1948	February	Communist coup in Czechoslovakia
	April	Organization of American States established
	May	United States recognizes Israel
	June	Berlin blockade begins; West mounts airlift
1949	April	North Atlantic Treaty signed
	May	Berlin blockade ends
	August	Soviet Union successfully tests atomic bomb
	September	Federal Republic of Germany established
	October	German Democratic Republic established
		Mao Zedong proclaims People's Republic of China; Chiang Kai-shek retreats to Taiwan
1950	February	Sino-Soviet Treaty of Alliance signed
		McCarthy denounces traitors in speech at Wheeling, West Virginia, and stimulates McCarthyism in United States
	April	NSC-68 recommends American rearmament
	June	North Korea invades South Korea and begins the Korean War
	November	China enters Korean War
1952	November	Eisenhower elected US president
1953	March	Death of Stalin
	July	Korean cease-fire signed
	September	Khrushchev becomes general secretary of the Soviet Communist Party
1954	April	Eisenhower describes 'domino theory' at press conference
	May	Vietminh defeat French army at Dien Bien Phu
	June	Guatemalan government overthrown by coup organized by Central Intelligence Agency
	July	Geneva Accords end First Indochina War; Vietnam is divided into North and South
	September	South East Asia Treaty Organization established to defend Far East

1955	April	Bandung Conference of neutral Asian and African nations
	May	West Germany joins North Atlantic Treaty Organization
		Warsaw Pact established
1956	February	Khrushchev denounces Stalin's 'cult of personality' at the Twentieth Congress of the Soviet Communist Party
	October	Soviet Union crushes uprising in Hungary
	November	Suez crisis
1957	January	Eisenhower Doctrine announced to defend Middle East
	March	Treaty of Rome formally establishes European Economic Community
	October	Soviet Union launches sputnik
		Second Indochina War begins
1958	November	Khrushchev initiates Berlin Crisis by threatening to sign a peace treaty with East Germany
1959	January	Castro rises to power in Cuba
1960	May	Paris summit meeting collapses over U-2 incident
	July	United Nations intervenes in Congo crisis
	November	Kennedy elected US president
1961	April	Bay of Pigs landing
	May	Kennedy sends Special Forces troops to South Vietnam
	June	Kennedy and Khruschev hold summit meeting in Vienna
	August	Berlin Wall built
		Alliance for Progress announced for Latin America
1962	October	Cuban Missile Crisis
1963	May	Organization of African Unity established
	August	Nuclear Test Ban Treaty signed
	November	Kennedy assassinated; Johnson becomes US president
1964	August	Johnson orders first air strikes on North Vietnam
	October	Khrushchev replaced by Brezhnev as general secretary of the Soviet Communist Party

		War
		Nixon issues global alert
1974	August	Nixon resigns as a result of Watergate scandal; Ford becomes US president
	September	Haile Selassie overthrown in Ethiopia
	November	Brezhnev and Ford meet at Vladivostok and agree to draft of SALT II treaty
1975	April	North Vietnamese troops capture Saigon; Second Indochina War ends in victory for North Vietnam
	August	Helsinki Accords signed
	November	Civil war breaks out in Angola
1976	September	Death of Mao Zedong
	November	Carter elected US president
1977	July	Ethiopia and Somalia go to war over disputed Ogaden territory
1979	January	US and China establish full diplomatic relations
	February	Shah of Iran overthrown
	June	Brezhnev and Carter sign SALT II treaty at Vienna summit meeting
	July	Sandinistas seize power in Nicaragua
	November	Iranian hostage crisis begins
	December	Soviet Union invades Afghanistan
1980	January	Carter Doctrine announced to defend Persian Gulf region
	August	Solidarity movement is formed in Poland
	November	Reagan elected US president
1981	January	American hostages in Iran released
1982	June	Strategic Arms Reduction Talks (START) begin in Geneva
	November	Death of Brezhnev: Andropov becomes general secretary of the Soviet Communist Party
1983	March	Reagan announces Strategic Defense Initiative
	October	Reagan orders military intervention in Grenada
1984	February	Death of Andropov; Chernenko becomes general secretary of the Soviet Communist Party
1985	March	Death of Chernenko; Gorbachev becomes

		general secretary of the Soviet Communist Party
	November	First Reagan–Gorbachev summit meeting in Geneva
1986	October	Reagan–Gorbachev summit meeting in Reykjavik
	November	Iran–Contra scandal revealed
1987	December	Reagan–Gorbachev summit meeting in Washington; Intermediate-Range and Shorter-Range Missiles Treaty signed
1988	May/June	Reagan visits Moscow
	November	Bush elected US president
1989	February	Soviet troops withdraw from Afghanistan
	June	Solidarity wins Polish parliamentary election
	August	Non-communist government takes power in Poland
	September	Hungary opens its borders to the West
	November	Berlin Wall opened
	December	Non-communist government takes power in Czechoslovakia
		Ceauşescu overthrown in Romania
		Bush–Gorbachev summit meeting in Malta
1990	March	Gorbachev elected president of the Soviet Union
	October	West and East Germany reunified
	November	CSCE Conference proclaims the end of the Cold War
1991	January	Persian Gulf War begins
	July	Bush and Gorbachev sign START I treaty
	August	Gorbachev resigns as general secretary of the Communist Party
	December	Soviet Union formally disbands and becomes the Commonwealth of Independent States

1

Beginning of the Cold War

Rise of the Superpowers

Despite their enormous geographical size, large populations and natural resources, the United States of America (USA, US or United States) and the Union of Soviet Socialist Republics (USSR or Soviet Union) assumed a peripheral role in international affairs in the period between the two world wars, from 1919 to 1939. American diplomats traditionally emphasized the separation of the 'New World' of the Americas from the 'Old World' of Europe and pursued a policy of avoiding political and military entanglements towards that continent which was generally described as 'isolationism'. Although a large part of the Soviet Union actually adjoined Europe, the communist state headed by Joseph Stalin, the general secretary of the Central Committee of the Communist Party from 1924 to 1953, was similarly suspicious of close contact with capitalist governments. According to the doctrine of Marxism-Leninism those countries formed an international system that was hostile to the existence of communism. Consequently, both the United States and the Soviet Union were diplomatic bystanders in the wrangles over territorial boundaries which increasingly wracked Europe during the 1930s. The great European powers of Britain, France, Germany and Italy were accustomed to dominating world affairs and their telegraph wires hummed as they squabbled among themselves over control of the Sudetenland and the Polish Corridor. When war ultimately erupted in September 1939, however, it quickly expanded beyond the continent of Europe and acquired global dimensions.

Just over two decades earlier, in 1917, the United States had become directly involved in the fighting in World War I as an ally of Britain and France. Led by the idealistic rhetoric of President Woodrow Wilson, the American people had characteristically sought 'to make the world safe for democracy'. But the peace settlement brought severe disillusionment. The traditional American aversion to entangling alliances with foreign countries was soon restored as the United States withdrew into isolationism and resolved to stay neutral in European disputes. The mistake of military intervention in an overseas war would not be repeated. 'Never again' became a popular slogan of the 1930s and was reaffirmed by the cries of 'America first' and 'Fortress America' in 1940.

Although the United States officially adopted the policy of neutrality in 1939, there was increasing anxiety among government officials that the whole of Europe might fall under the control of the fascist dictators, Adolf Hitler of Germany and Benito Mussolini of Italy. President Franklin D. Roosevelt sought to alert American opinion to the attendant dangers when he stressed the urgent need to defend the 'four freedoms' of speech, worship, freedom from want, and freedom from fear. 'We Americans are vitally concerned in your defense of freedom', Roosevelt told the democratic nations of the world in January 1941. In what would later become known as the policy of 'lend-lease', he added: 'We are putting forth our energies, our resources and our organizing powers to give you the strength to regain and maintain a free world. We shall send you, in ever-increasing numbers, ships, planes, tanks, guns' (Siracusa, 1978, p. 5). Despite Roosevelt's apparently unequivocal pledge of support for the countries fighting against the fascist powers, the United States still hesitated to enter the war formally. The surprise attack by Japan on the American naval base at Pearl Harbor in December 1941 and Germany's declaration of war on the United States only a few days later brought, however, an abrupt end to the period of American neutrality.

Whereas Roosevelt was openly critical of the Nazi regime in Germany, Stalin adopted a more ambiguous attitude and initially viewed the crisis over Poland as an opportunity to expand Soviet territorial borders to the west. The Non-Aggression Pact was signed with Germany in August 1939 and allowed the Soviet Union to seize the Baltic states and part of eastern Poland. Moreover, Stalin was not unhappy to see the capitalist powers fight among themselves. Not only did this bring immediate territorial gains but it hastened the prospect of the complete collapse of capitalism which would lead inevitably, as the doctrine of Marxism-Leninism predicted, to the victory of international communism. But Stalin appeared guilty of miscalculation and military unpreparedness when Germany launched a massive invasion of the Soviet Union in June 1941. An epic struggle for national survival ensued in which the Soviet leader was soon pleading with the West for assistance.

Despite having established diplomatic relations with the Soviet Union in 1933, Americans were traditionally hostile to communism. It was viewed as an alien ideology that ruthlessly suppressed political, economic and religious freedom. But the prospect of Adolf Hitler and the Nazis gaining control over Europe was even more alarming. In the immediate aftermath of the attack on Pearl Harbor, Americans had instinctively demanded massive military retaliation against Japan. Roosevelt and his advisers, however, regarded Nazi Germany as the greater danger and consequently insisted on pursuing a Europe-first military strategy while a 'holding operation' was conducted against Japan. American troops were rushed to Britain and Stalin was led to believe that a 'second front' against the Germans would be speedily opened in Western Europe. But this was not judged to be militarily feasible until the Normandy landings in 1944. The delay led to Soviet complaints and later recriminations against the West that they had been deliberately left on their own to fight the Nazi war machine. In the meantime, however, American assistance took another form. By recommending that lend-lease be extended to the Soviet Union, Roosevelt showed his agreement with the British prime minister, Winston Churchill, that Stalin was 'a welcome guest at [a] hungry table' (Dallek, 1979, p. 293). Soon it would be argued that the United States and the Soviet Union were not only fighting on the same side but also shared a common desire to promote world peace, prosperity and democracy. The mutual fear of Nazi Germany had thereby brought together an improbable 'Grand Alliance' of the 'Big Three' powers comprising the forces of British imperialism, American capitalism and Soviet communism.

The ensuing global struggle was one of total war in which the superior resources of the Big Three assured them ultimate military victory. In fact, a new historical epoch was under way. After the self-destruction caused by the 'Thirty Years War' from 1914 to 1945, the fortunes of a weak and divided Europe were to be dictated by powers outside the mainstream of previous European history. In 1945 Germany and Italy were defeated nations. Their economies were devastated and their people cowed by foreign military occupation and administration. France was liberated, but was only belatedly admitted to the circle of the great powers. This recognition was grudgingly given by the Big Three and could scarcely hide the scars of French military defeat, economic stagnation and the mood of national humiliation and bitterness brought about by the Vichy regime and its discredited policy of wartime collaboration with the Germans.

After standing alone against the might of Nazi Germany in 1940–41, Britain emerged from the war with considerable pride and a sense of achievement. British courage was personified by Winston Churchill, whose international reputation was at its zenith. The British prime minister deservedly took the centre of the world stage along with Roosevelt and Stalin. Signs of Britain's relative decline as a great power were, however, apparent throughout the war and were merely disguised by the euphoria of victory in 1945. Churchill had desperately sought American assistance in 1940 because he believed it was the only way to ensure the survival of the British empire. American intervention did secure eventual military victory over the fascist powers but at the price of accelerating Britain's economic and military subordination to the United States. Furthermore, the enormous cost of war compelled Britain to incur vast new debts and liquidate so much of its overseas assets that a superpower role was beyond British resources. Postwar events such as the urgent need for an American loan and the granting of independence to India in 1947 symbolized the passing of an era. However, the transition was not always clearly perceived by contemporaries and was masked by Britain's retention of a large colonial empire, substantial military forces including the development of atomic weapons, and the claim to a 'special relationship' with the United States based upon a shared history, language and values. Consequently, for some time actual British power and influence in international affairs were considerably overestimated by America, by Russia and by Britain itself.

The Soviet Union suffered the heaviest losses of any country during the war and was economically crippled in 1945. More than

20 million people had died, while agriculture and industry lay devastated. Only by supreme military, economic and personal sacrifice had the Soviet people rolled back the Nazi war machine to the German capital itself. The struggle was aptly named 'the Great Patriotic War against Fascism'. Not only was Mother Russia saved, but the dramatic eclipse of Nazi Germany also created a vacuum of power in Eastern Europe so that the Soviet Union found itself in a position of unaccustomed and almost complete dominance in the region. Under the leadership of Stalin, the Soviet Union soon demonstrated to the West that it possessed the necessary political will and organization to direct its military power, human resources and economic potential to merit the status of a world superpower.

The advance of the Soviet Union was overshadowed by the even more remarkable rise of the United States from isolation to world leadership. In marked contrast to the other belligerents', American wartime losses and sacrifices were disproportionately small. Indeed, the United States might be said actually to have benefited from the war. Not only had population increased from 131 million to 140 million, but the gross national product had soared from $90 billion in 1939 to $211 billion in 1945. The United States had replaced Britain as indisputably the world's leading economic power and supplier of financial credit. Moreover, it possessed a vast military establishment which in 1945 also acquired the monopoly of atomic weapons. Although he feared that, once the war had ended, the American people would desire a return to the traditional policy of isolationism, President Roosevelt firmly believed that America both needed and was obliged to restore the world to peace and prosperity. It was a vision of the future which he frequently proclaimed in his public speeches and statements.

The American president understood, however, that diplomacy did not operate in a vacuum and that the United States must take into account the views of other nations. During the war itself, Roosevelt had considered military cooperation between the Big Three to be so crucial for victory that he either avoided or tactfully ignored potential disagreements. A friendly atmosphere pervaded the summit meetings held at Tehran in 1943 and at Yalta in the Crimea in February 1945. The president was particularly keen to establish a special personal relationship with the Soviet leader. The journeys were extremely long and tiring, but the results were pleasing. On his return from Tehran, Roosevelt told the American people: 'I got along fine with Marshal Stalin . . . and I believe that we are going to get along very well with him and the Russian people – very well indeed' (Dallek, 1979, p. 439). The image later assiduously promoted in the American media of Stalin as a kindly 'Uncle Joe' was intended to be reassuring and implied that the prospects for future cooperation were bright.

Roosevelt did not reveal publicly, however, that he had given Stalin what amounted to a recognition that Eastern Europe was a Soviet sphere of influence. The advance of the Red Army into Poland brought this matter into prominence in 1944. Churchill stressed the importance of restoring Polish freedom and reminded his wartime partners that Britain and France had gone to war against Germany over this very issue in 1939. But Poland was also the historic gateway to Moscow for foreign invaders. Stalin was in no mood to compromise over what he described as 'not only a question of honor for Russia, but one of life and death' (Dallek, 1979, p. 513). The Soviet leader insisted on retaining the areas of eastern Poland which he had gained from the Non-Aggression Pact signed with Hitler in 1939. Territorial compensation would be given to Poland by pushing its western border across Germany to the line of the Oder–Neisse rivers. Moreover, Stalin would not permit the automatic return to power of the non-communist Polish prewar political leaders who had escaped from the Nazis and found exile in London.

Despite British grumbles, the Americans remained quiescent and tacitly allowed the extension of communist control over Poland. Roosevelt evidently wished to avoid making that country a divisive issue between the allies. In fact, there was little else that could be done so long as Poland was occupied by the Red Army and allied troops were hundreds of miles away. In February 1945 the subject appeared to be resolved at the Yalta conference by the 'Declaration on Liberated Europe', which sought to provide for 'free and unfettered elections' in the territories liberated from Nazi tyranny. But this merely proved to be a face-saving diplomatic compromise that allowed both sides to interpret 'democracy' in the way that best suited themselves. Poland provided a prime example. The Soviet authorities made token gestures of permitting members of the exiled Polish government in London to return to Poland and take up political activities, but communists remained firmly in control of the country.

In effect, the elation of imminent victory over Germany moderated latent dissensions at the Yalta conference. Roosevelt appeared more interested in affairs in the Far East and was pleased to secure Stalin's agreement that the Soviet Union would join the war against Japan three months after the defeat of Germany. In discussions concerning Europe the president was unwilling to give any definite postwar commitments and implied that America would speedily disengage militarily from the European continent. In his opinion, the United States was not a European power and its troops would be out of Europe within two years after the end of the war. The implication was that Churchill and Stalin would be left to decide between themselves the exact nature of Europe's fate.

American policy, however, was ambivalent. Roosevelt's private acknowledgment of the existence of distinct British and Soviet spheres of influence was contradicted by his public speeches, which stressed Wilsonian ideas of 'open' diplomacy and an insistence on the right of self-determination for all peoples, including those of the liberated nations of Eastern Europe, to choose their own form of government. American idealism was also characteristically mixed with a self-serving realism. While America might choose to run down its military power after the war, it was evident that there was no intention of surrendering its new-found world influence. 'If we are to measure up to the task of peace with the same stature as we have measured up to the task of war,' declared Roosevelt in the closing months of the war, 'we must see that the institutions of peace rest firmly on the solid foundations of international political and economic cooperation' (Schlesinger, 1983, I, p. 17). The president posited a concept of a liberal-capitalist world order headed by newly created international institutions such as the United Nations Organization, International Monetary Fund and World Bank, which would promote and guarantee world security and recovery. Under American tutelage, the Big Three would work together in this common endeavour.

Two months after the end of the fighting in Europe the victorious allies met in July 1945 at Potsdam near Berlin. Since the previous conference at Yalta, however, there had been a significant change of personnel in the composition of the Big Three. A new American president had taken office. Roosevelt had died in April and was succeeded by Harry Truman. The result of national elections in Britain meant that the newly elected British prime minister, Clement

Attlee, replaced Churchill during the meeting. Only Stalin remained to give personal continuity with the past. Nevertheless, the rhetoric of wartime alliance was reaffirmed by all three leaders. The task of winning the war was over, but a common desire existed to ensure peace and to avoid a third world war. The defeated enemy powers anxiously awaited the decisions on their fate that were to be decided at councils from which they were absent. In principle, the super-powers were in agreement, but serious difficulties quickly surfaced over the future of Germany.

The Problem of Germany

In the spring of 1945 the Third Reich was effectively abolished, when the advancing armies of the Big Three triumphantly joined together on the plains of Germany. The victors found themselves presiding over a nation in ruins and a people in despair. Despite the local chaos and desolation, the transition from war to peace proceeded more smoothly than expected. Germany was placed under military rule and divided into geographical zones broadly reflecting the actual positions drawn up at the close of hostilities by the occupying armies. The Russians were stationed in the east and the Americans took the south while the British established them-selves in the northwest. The main agricultural region was therefore controlled by the Soviets while the industrial heartland of the Ruhr was allocated to Britain. A later quip was that the Americans were left with the scenery. On the insistence of Britain and the United States, France was given parts of the British and American zones. The city of Berlin was similarly divided into four separate sectors and became the headquarters of the Four-power Allied Control Council which was formally established to rule Germany.

The goal and priority of the Big Three during the war had been to bring about the military defeat of Germany. There was, however, no such clear purpose regarding the postwar future of that country. The problem was simply too complex and too important to permit of a quick solution. Moreover, in contrast to the case in Poland or Japan, no one single power possessed a preponderating military influence in Germany. As a result it proved impossible to maintain German territorial integrity and national unity. Although the imposition of separate zones of occupation was both practical and administratively sensible, it was regarded as a temporary arrangement pending the organization of a full-scale international conference to effect a definitive peace treaty. The onus was upon the Big Three, especially the two superpowers, to work together to achieve a settlement that would have a crucial effect upon the future political reconstruction of Europe and the preservation of world peace.

In 1945 a general belief prevailed among the victors that the German people had been treated too leniently at the end of World War I and that this mistake should not be repeated. 'The fact that they are a defeated nation, collectively and individually,' President Roosevelt declared, 'must be so impressed upon them that they will hesitate to start any new war' (Dallek, 1979, p. 472). An understandable instinct to take revenge and mete out punishment was evident in the denazification programmes which were rapidly instituted within each zone. High-ranking Nazis faced the severest penalties while thousands of lesser government officials were treated as criminals and shown little sympathy.

Linked to the question of punishment was the common desire of the Big Three to prevent the resurgence of Germany as a future military threat. They were unanimous that the German armed forces should be immediately disbanded. Some consideration was also briefly given at the wartime conferences to dismembering Germany into several smaller and separate states. Although the Big Three recognized that Germany must lose territory in the east to the Soviet Union and Poland, they demonstrated no desire for further territorial aggrandizement at Germany's expense. The temporary nature of the zonal division was reaffirmed and it was anticipated that Germany would soon be reunified as a single nation state.

The debate over economic policy was more controversial and ultimately proved divisive. Although they agreed that Germany should be kept economically weak, the powers were uncertain how this was to be achieved. The American secretary of the Treasury, Henry Morgenthau, had argued in 1944 that Germany be 'deindustrialized' and savagely reduced to what amounted to a medieval pastoral economy. The 'Morgenthau Plan' never became official American policy, but its influence was reflected in the decision to regard the German people as a captured enemy nation who should expect to be maintained at no more than a low standard of living for the immediate future.

The outlines of a common economic strategy emerged as the Big Three agreed to dismantle Germany's warmaking industries and to restrict economic production to low levels so as to allow only a minimal standard of living for the local populace. But implementation of this policy quickly became entangled with Stalin's insistence that large reparations also be exacted from Germany, in the shape of the removal of industrial equipment and transfer of raw materials to assist Soviet domestic reconstruction. At the Yalta conference in February 1945 Foreign Minister Vyacheslav M. Molotov proposed that Germany be required to pay reparations of $20 billion of which the Soviet Union would receive half.

Not having suffered bombing and invasion the Americans felt no need of reparations, and were lukewarm to an idea which they believed had not only proved financially counter-productive and politically troublesome during the 1920s but also contributed directly to the rise to power of Hitler and the ensuing world war. Moreover, if the United States wished Germany to recover economically, a policy of rehabilitation rather than repression was more appropriate. Officials at the State Department urged the former while the Treasury and the War Department favoured the latter. When this issue was raised during the war President Roosevelt had appeared uncertain and provided no clear direction. He preferred to concentrate on winning the war. Until that was achieved, awkward political decisions were best postponed.

Nevertheless, while the United States wanted no reparations from Germany for itself, they could hardly be denied the Soviets after that country's immense wartime sacrifices. Roosevelt admitted as much at the Yalta conference although his untimely death in April 1945 meant that the actual task of working out a formal reparations agreement fell to his successor, Harry Truman. The new president was inexperienced in foreign affairs and did not attempt to disguise his personal hostility towards communism. Nevertheless, he was willing to agree in principle to Germany having to pay reparations to the victims of its aggression.

In practice, American officials believed that they possessed considerable bargaining power over the Soviets since the latter were desperate for the industrial goods and equipment which were largely located in the Ruhr. At the Potsdam conference in July 1945 Secretary of State James Byrnes declined, therefore, to name an exact total figure for reparations. Instead, he worked out a compromise in which the Soviets would draw the bulk of reparations from their own zone while being given only limited amounts of industrial material from the west. The outcome signified the American desire to restrict if not exclude Soviet contact with the western zones. In effect, Germany was being partitioned by the superpowers. This was implicit in the question posed by Molotov to Byrnes: 'Would not the Secretary's suggestion mean that each country would have a free hand in their own zones and would act entirely independently of the others?' Byrnes acknowledged that 'the Soviet Union would take what it wished from its own zone' (Kuklick, 1972, p. 155).

In contrast to the harsh reparations policy favoured by the Soviets, the American military authorities soon adopted a humane and sympathetic attitude towards the defeated enemy. 'God, I hate the Germans', General Dwight Eisenhower had once written, but the sight of American GIs distributing candy bars and chewing gum to German children made him relax the regulations prohibiting the fraternization of American troops with the local population (Ambrose, 1983b, pp. 422–3). Although the policy agreed at the Potsdam conference required that the German living standard be kept low, American officials became alarmed by the growing evidence of suffering arising from shortages of food and fuel in their zone. The dilemma was compounded by the onset of winter and the daily arrival of thousands of refugees fleeing from the east, the vast majority of whom were destitute and starving. Furthermore, the lack of local agricultural capacity compelled the American authorities to resort to importing food and raw materials from the United States. Not only was this expensive, but unless steps were taken to revive the Germany economy it threatened to become an intolerable burden for the American taxpayer.

The American deputy military governor, General Lucius Clay, considered that the food crisis could only become worse unless a centralized administrative agency was established to ensure the efficient interzonal allocation and distribution of economic resources. In his view the major stumbling block was not so much the Soviets as France. The latter sought to keep Germany permanently weak not only by joining the Soviets in demanding heavy reparations but also in resisting all attempts to make the Allied Control Council in Berlin an effective instrument of central government. In May 1946 a frustrated General Clay sought to force governmental discussion of the whole issue by unilaterally halting the transfer of reparations from the American zone. While France still remained silently intransigent, the Soviets were stung into protesting that Clay's action was illegal.

A constructive response, however, was forthcoming from Britain, whose government shared American suspicions that the Soviets were using the reparations issue to keep Germany economically weak and consequently vulnerable to communist subversion and ultimate control. Moreover, faced with the same dilemma as the United States in having to feed the German people in its zone, Britain regarded joint economic action as the quickest means to mitigate an escalating financial burden. Britain also desperately needed American dollars to finance imports while the United States required supplies of coal and raw materials from the British zone. Anglo-American cooperation was formalized in mid-1946 by the decision to combine their two zones into a separate economic unit. The new entity was called 'Bizonia' and came into being in January 1947.

At the Yalta conference in February 1945 President Roosevelt had predicted that American troops would be withdrawn from Europe within two years of the end of the war. Eighteen months later Secretary of State Byrnes made an important speech at Stuttgart in which he indicated that the Potsdam agreement concerning Germany had broken down. The United States had withdrawn into isolationism in 1919, but Byrnes warned: 'We will not again make that mistake. We intend to continue our interest in the affairs of Europe and of the world' (Schlesinger, 1983, I, p. 436). The implication that Germany was to be rehabilitated and not repressed was underlined by Byrnes's successor, General George Marshall, who noted in March 1947 that his government 'is opposed to policies which will continue Germany as a congested slum or an economic poorhouse in the center of Europe' (Schlesinger, 1983, I, p. 459). In effect, the United States was prepared to lead and finance the economic reconstruction of Germany in order to provide a buffer against Soviet expansion.

Clay's virtual ultimatum in May 1946 had brought an end to the frustrating saga of reparations. Indeed, Brynes's spoiling tactics had proved effective. The Soviets felt aggrieved since no more than $25 million to $50 million in goods was actually transferred from the western zones to the Soviet Union. To add insult to injury, the

Western powers accused the Soviets of systematic looting of the eastern zone. Further discord was evident in the meetings of foreign ministers held at Moscow in March 1947 and later at London in November. The resulting diplomatic impasse meant that the great peace conference to decide the future of Germany was abandoned. Instead, the temporary military boundaries drawn up in 1945 became fixed borders in 1949 when the French zone joined with Bizonia. The subsequent division of Germany into two separate and hostile countries underlined the state of acute rivalry between the two superpowers and demonstrated that the wartime partnership could not survive the transition into peacetime.

The Containment of Communism

The conflict between the superpowers over Germany was mirrored elsewhere, especially in Eastern Europe and the Middle East. The establishment of a communist government in Poland aroused American charges that Stalin had ruthlessly gone back on his undertaking given at the Yalta conference to allow 'free elections' in that country. The issue was bluntly raised by Truman at his notorious and well-publicized first meeting as president with Molotov in April 1945. 'I have never been talked to like that in my life', complained the Soviet foreign minister. Truman brusquely retorted: 'Carry out your agreements and you won't get talked to like that' (Truman, 1955, p. 85). An official response was soon forthcoming from Stalin which tersely declared that 'the Soviet Government cannot agree to the existence in Poland of a Government hostile to it' (Siracusa, 1978, p. 80). Soviet security considerations were hardly to be swayed by the words of the American president no matter how tough they might sound.

The United States was able, however, to exert more tangible influence in the crisis which emerged over Iran. That country had been under joint Anglo-Soviet military occupation since 1941 and both nations had agreed to withdraw their forces by March 1946. Reports of Soviet troops staying on in the northern province of Azerbaijan to aid a separatist movement against the rule of the shah of Iran suggested, however, that Stalin intended to violate the wartime understanding. But the question really at issue was control of the region's valuable oil resources. 'Our continued access to oil in the Middle East is especially threatened by Soviet penetration into Iran', noted one White House official (Krock, 1968, p. 471). Consequently, a remote part of the world suddenly acquired international significance as an alarmed Truman administration determined to resist what was perceived as deliberate Soviet aggression. American diplomatic support was given to the shah's decision to send Iranian troops to the northern border and also to raise the issue at the United Nations. Secretary of State Byrnes seized the opportunity to go before the Security Council and publicly condemn Soviet imperialism. Although the Soviet representative, Andrei Gromyko, chose to stage a dramatic walkout from the chamber, the Soviets quickly defused the crisis by agreeing to abide by the wartime agreement and pull out their military forces from Iran in May 1946.

The vigorous American response to events in Iran reflected the growing conviction in Washington that the Soviet Union was becoming an enemy of the United States and that its insatiable appetite for expansion must be checked. Especially influential were the ideas of George Kennan, an experienced career diplomat serving as chargé d'affaires at the American embassy in Moscow. In February 1946 he dispatched to the State Department what became known as the 'Long Telegram'. In it he warned of the danger of 'acting chummy' with the Soviets and explained that their leaders could not be trusted because they were Marxist-Leninists and 'committed fanatically to the belief that with [the] US there can be no permanent modus vivendi' (Kennan, 1968, pp. 291, 557). The analysis merely confirmed and reinforced the already strong anti-Soviet prejudices of many Washington officials. A special report prepared for President Truman during the summer of 1946 by his White House aide, Clark Clifford, stated that 'compromise and concessions are considered by the Soviets, to be evidence of weakness'. Clifford's sobering conclusion was that the United States must avoid the error of 'appeasement' and should even be prepared to go to war if necessary to resist Stalin's ambitions for world conquest (Krock, 1968, pp. 477–8).

The changing mood in the United States towards involvement in world affairs was indicated by the passage of the National Security Act in July 1947. The principal purpose of the act was to improve the flow of information and advice to the president by creating the National Security Council (NSC) to advise on foreign policy and the Central Intelligence Agency (CIA) to gather and interpret foreign 'intelligence'. The CIA was also assigned the function of undertaking overseas 'covert' operations. In addition, the armed services were united within a Department of Defense whose headquarters were located in the Pentagon just outside Washington DC. The beginning of what would later be called the 'national security state' coincided appropriately with the appearance in July 1947 of an important article by George Kennan that publicized many of the ideas contained in his 'Long Telegram' and notably stressed the need for 'a long-term, patient but firm and vigilant containment of Russian expansive tendencies' (Kennan, 1968, p. 359). The term 'containment' was soon widely adopted to describe the aim of American policy in its dealings with the Soviet Union.

In fact, the attention of the American public had already been drawn to the new strategy by events in Iran and especially the eastern Mediterranean. This latter area was traditionally regarded as within the British sphere of influence, until the British government secretly informed the State Department on 21 February 1947 that it could no longer afford to sustain a substantial economic and military role in Greece and Turkey beyond 31 March. The spectre of Soviet aggression loomed large in the minds of Washington officials who feared that communists were responsible for the civil war that was currently raging in Greece. Moreover, American suspicions of a conspiracy masterminded from Moscow appeared to be confirmed by simultaneous pressure from Stalin on the Turkish government to secure rights of naval access for Soviet warships to the Mediterranean.

A sense of urgency and excitement permeated the inner circle of the Truman administration. It was decided that prompt and decisive action was necessary to help Greece and Turkey. But doubts were expressed whether the American public and Congress would support the United States openly replacing Britain in a distant area of the world where Americans historically had little national interest or direct involvement. Consequently, the communist bogy was deliberately overstated to alert congressional and public opinion to the danger. The lines of battle between East and West were eloquently drawn by Truman in his address to Congress on 12 March 1947:

> At the present moment in world history nearly every nation must choose between alternative ways of life. The choice is too often not

a free one. One way of life is based upon the will of the majority, and is distinguished by free institutions, representative government, free elections, guarantees of individual liberty, freedom of speech and religion and freedom from political oppression. The second way of life is based upon the will of a minority forcibly imposed on the majority. It relies upon terror and oppression, a controlled press and radio, framed elections and the suppression of personal freedoms. I believe that it must be the policy of the United States to support free peoples who are resisting attempted subjugation by armed minorities or by outside pressures. (Halle, 1967, p. 120)

Congress speedily assented to Truman's request for the relatively small amount of $400 million to 'save' Greece and Turkey from communism. But the unilateral pledge of American support to 'free peoples' had much wider ramifications. The president's speech was referred to as the 'Truman Doctrine' and its impact and significance soon extended far beyond the eastern Mediterranean. The same affliction of poverty, which bred despair and undermined democratic institutions in Greece, was also perceived as present throughout Western Europe. State Department officials carefully observed the political activities of communist parties, especially in France and Italy. They feared that total economic collapse was imminent and would be followed by political chaos and revolution. In April 1947 Secretary of State Marshall returned from a visit to Europe with the gloomy diagnosis that 'the patient is sinking while the doctors deliberate' (Halle, 1967, p. 167). A massive programme of external financial aid was urgently required to stimulate economic revival and thereby relieve the sense of hopelessness and anxiety that encouraged and facilitated communist encroachment. In a speech at Harvard University on 5 June Marshall announced his government's intention to promote the economic recovery of Europe. 'It is logical', he declared, 'that the United States should do whatever it is able to do to assist in the return of normal economic health in the world, without which there can be no political stability and no assured peace' (Schlesinger, 1983, I, p. 53).

The funding of the recovery programme was estimated at several billions of dollars and would require the approval of an American Congress that not only was strongly economy-minded but also contained a Republican majority. Passage was therefore by no means guaranteed. A public relations campaign ensued in which administration officials sought to remove American party politics from the issue by emphasizing its 'bipartisan' political character. They highlighted the extreme gravity of Europe's economic plight and how this seriously jeopardized the stability of democratic governments throughout that continent. Calculated appeals were also made to American economic self-interest by pointing out that increased trade would directly benefit American exports. Congressmen, who were concerned about the cost of the programme, were reassured by statements that American financial assistance would be contingent upon European cooperation and self-help.

Led by the governments of Britain and France, the countries of Western Europe enthusiastically welcomed what the British foreign minister, Ernest Bevin, later described as 'a lifeline to sinking men' (*New York Times*, 2 April 1949). Faced with acute shortages of food and fuel, rising inflation and a projected annual deficit in balance of payments of more than \$5 billion, Europe was desperate for American dollars to finance trade and investment. French concern surfaced, however, over American insistence that Germany be included in the recovery plan. 'Without a revival of German production,' affirmed Kennan, 'there can be no revival of Europe's economy' (LaFeber, 1976, p. 63). The need for immediate aid and the tacit promise that substantial sums would be specially earmarked for France persuaded the latter to acquiesce in Germany's inclusion.

Even more controversial was the prospect of Soviet participation. Although the recovery programme was intended to contain communist expansion, Marshall had initially stressed that it was open to all European countries, including those presently under communist governments: 'Our policy is directed not against any country or doctrine but against hunger, poverty, desperation and chaos' (Schlesinger, 1983, I, p. 53). Indeed, the Soviets took Marshall at his word and accepted the invitation made by the foreign ministers of Britain and France to attend a Three-power preliminary conference to discuss the American proposals. In June 1947 Molotov arrived at Paris accompanied by no fewer than 89 advisers. It seemed that the Soviets regarded the Marshall Plan as a serious alternative to German reparations. But the aid was not without strings because inclusion in the recovery programme would require participants to disclose information about their economies to the United States. The implied prospect of American supervision and interference in the Soviet economy was unacceptable to Molotov.

After only a few days he abruptly withdrew from the conference accusing the United States of a plot to infringe the sovereignty of independent nations. In his opinion, the proposed scheme was a cunning attempt to rescue American capitalism by economically enslaving Europe.

The Soviets also saw the Marshall Plan as a real threat to their control of Eastern Europe. Poland, Czechoslovakia and Hungary had already expressed their intention to attend the full-scale conference to be held at Paris in late July. Pressure was now applied from Moscow to persuade those governments to join the Soviet Union in boycotting the meeting. The Soviets proceeded to stage their own rival conference in September at which the Communist Information Bureau (Cominform) was created, comprising the Soviet Union, Poland, Czechoslovakia, Hungary, Romania, Bulgaria, Yugoslavia and the communist parties of France and Italy. The 'democratic' nations of the Cominform declared that they were united in their fight against American 'imperialism'.

Meanwhile, the other European nations had accepted the British and French invitations to assemble at Paris in July 1947 to consider the Marshall Plan. The deliberate absence of the communist countries was not unwelcome to Ernest Bevin who had initially feared that the Soviets would play the destructive role of 'a Trojan horse' (Bartlett, 1994, p. 266). Within ten weeks a comprehensive scheme was drawn up for the economic recovery of Western Europe. In December Truman requested a congressional appropriation of $17 billion to fund the European Recovery Programme (ERP). Although the desire to help Western Europe was very evident, the Republican majority hesitated to grant such huge spending powers to a Democratic administration. However, doubts were dramatically dispelled by the communist coup in Czechoslovakia in February 1948. The deliberate and successful use of intimidation to force the resignation of the coalition government sent shock waves through Washington and highlighted the urgent need to aid democratic forces in Western Europe. 'Prompt passage' of the recovery programme, Truman informed Congress, 'is the most telling contribution we can now make toward peace.' The vote to implement the Marshall Plan was regarded as putting the 'Truman Doctrine in action'. The president solemnly concluded: 'We must be prepared to pay the price of peace, or assuredly we shall pay the price of war' (Schlesinger, 1983, I, pp. 128–9; Yergin, 1978,

p. 321). Comfortable majorities were forthcoming in both Houses of Congress. One of the costs, however, was the division and subsequent consolidation of Europe into two competing and hostile camps.

Historical Debate over the Origins of the Cold War

The Cold War was the dominant issue in international affairs during the second half of the twentieth century. Over several decades the world was effectively divided into two competing halves as the two superpowers and their allies engaged in a 'war of words' in which they ritually denounced the other side for both causing and perpetuating the conflict. Denied open access to their own diplomatic archives, Soviet historians have faithfully adhered to their government's 'official' version of events. A much more diverse approach has been forthcoming from American historians, reflecting their country's pluralistic and open society. Although Western European scholars have made a valuable contribution, historical research on the Cold War has been largely conducted by American historians, with the result that an American perspective – placing the United States at the centre of events – has dominated the literature and debate on the subject.

It is natural that many American writers have emphasized the special significance of the Cold War in modern world history because it represented a period in which their own country's military, economic and cultural power was so considerable and pervasive. A popular theme is to depict America's rise to global power as historically inevitable. One of the most frequently cited sources is the French traveller, Alexis de Tocqueville, who predicted as early as the 1830s that the destiny of the world would ultimately fall under the sway of the peoples of America and Russia (Halle, 1967). According to this linear view of history, the United States was simply assuming the leadership of Western civilization against the forces of Eastern barbarism. Western European scholars have acknowledged the power and the pre-eminent international role adopted by the United States after 1941, but tend to be less inclined to accord special or 'unique' importance to the Cold War. From their longer historical perspective it appears as yet another 'short episode' in the struggle for power and territory endemic in the history of modern Europe (Dunbabin, 1994, p. 478; Calvocoressi, 1982, p. 15). The end of the Cold War has given added validity to this view.

The exact timing of the beginning of the conflict has attracted debate. Some American writers have seen the struggle as a straightforward ideological battle of democracy versus communism, whose historical roots date back to the rise to power of the Bolsheviks in 1917 (Fleming, 1961). Crucial significance is assigned to President Woodrow Wilson's public condemnation of the Bolshevist government and his sending of American troops to Russia in 1918 to assist the futile efforts to restore the imperial regime. The wartime partnership between Roosevelt and Stalin is seen as an aberration which derived solely from the mutual desire to defeat Nazi Germany. Ideological rivalry resumed once this objective was achieved and was made even more acute and dangerous by the fact that the end of World War II brought American and Soviet armies face to face in Central Europe (Kennan, 1968).

The claim that the Cold War originated in 1917 is undermined by the fact that neither the United States nor the Soviet Union was a leading military power during the 1920s and 1930s. Consequently, their mutual antagonism was not translated into a military conflict that seriously threatened world peace. While not entirely ignoring the background of unfriendly relations, most historical investigation attaches fundamental importance to events occurring in Europe during the mid-1940s and considers those particular years as marking the beginning of the Cold War between East and West. The conventional view among American politicians and diplomats at the time was that the Soviet Union sought world domination. Stalin was accused of deliberately plotting a monolithic communist conspiracy, beginning with his refusal to allow free elections in Poland in contravention of the agreements made at the Yalta conference in 1945. Communist control was subsequently imposed throughout Eastern Europe and probes were made against Iran, Turkey and Greece. Western democracy was perceived to be in dire peril. Consequently, the United States was compelled to adopt the policy of containment exemplified in the Truman Doctrine and the Marshall Plan. This contemporary view that Stalin's aggressiveness was responsible for causing the Cold War has been endorsed by many historians in the West and represents the 'orthodox' or 'traditional' American interpretation 'that the Cold War was the brave and essential response of free men to communist aggression' (Schlesinger, 1967, p. 23; Spanier, 1960; Feis, 1970). The importance of the Truman Doctrine in articulating American aims and values has led to the citing of the president's speech in March 1947 as representing the beginning of the Cold War (Gaddis, 1974). In fact, it was also in 1947 that the term 'Cold War' first emerged in the United States as a result of a book with that title written by the influential journalist, Walter Lippmann.

Soviet writers have agreed on the importance of the Truman Doctrine in contributing to the conflict between East and West, but they regard their country's response as defensive and have singled out American imperialism as the cause of the Cold War (Ponomaryov et al., 1974). Their analysis has reflected an 'official' line which was maintained throughout the period of the Cold War. For example, Soviet news agencies criticized the Truman Doctrine only a day after it was enunciated as 'a smokescreen for expansion'. The United States government was believed to be under the control of 'Wall Street bosses', who sought to use American power to gain world economic supremacy. 'Alarmed by the achievements of Socialism in the U.S.S.R. . . . and by the post-war growth of the labor and democratic movements in all countries,' explained Andrei Zhadanov at the founding of the Cominform in 1947, 'the American reactionaries are disposed to take upon themselves the mission of "saviors" of the capitalist system from Communism' (Schlesinger, 1983, II, pp. 315, 353). The Marshall Plan was similarly regarded as an American plot to encircle the Soviet Union with hostile capitalist states. In addition, the United States was accused of endangering Soviet security by remilitarizing West Germany (Kennedy-Pipe, 1995, p. 121). The Soviet Union reacted to American provocation by maintaining control of Eastern Europe and creating its own system of political, economic and military alliances.

In the United States the 'orthodox' view held sway until the 1960s when it was vigorously challenged by the emergence of the 'revisionist' school of American historians. The new thinking reflected the findings resulting from the opening of American diplomatic archives covering the 1940s. It also mirrored the widespread disillusionment with President Lyndon Johnson's justification of the Vietnam War that raised an uncomfortable parallel with Truman's calculated use of the communist bogy in his appeal for aid to Greece and Turkey in 1947. In fact, the 'credibility gap' of the 1960s brought into question many of the assumptions underlying the 'orthodox' view. A prescriptive element was injected into the historical debate with the argument that American diplomacy towards Southeast Asia must avoid repeating the mistakes of the past. A prominent 'revisionist' theme was the adoption of a markedly sympathetic view of Soviet behaviour and the contention that Stalin's policies had been misperceived and misunderstood by the Truman administration. 'Revisionists' pointed out that, far from being untrustworthy, the Soviet leader had repeatedly proved himself a reliable wartime ally of the United States. Attention was also drawn to the military and economic weakness of the Soviet Union in the late 1940s. So great was Soviet insecurity that it was sensible for Stalin to insist on the establishment of friendly governments in neighbouring states. Stalin, therefore, was motivated by caution rather than aggression. Indeed, the 'revisionists' argued that American pressure provoked him into hostility towards the West and thereby precipitated the Cold War (Horowitz, 1965; Paterson, 1979; Ambrose, 1983a).

The succession to Roosevelt by Truman in April 1945 is seen as especially significant by 'revisionists' (Williams, 1962; Kolko, 1968; Paterson, 1988). Whereas Roosevelt carefully cultivated a friendly personal relationship with Stalin, Truman adopted a blustering tone, telling the Soviets to 'go to hell', and that agreements with that government had been 'a one-way street' (Bernstein, 1970, p. 26). The language and actions of the Truman administration were presented as unequivocally threatening to the Soviet Union. Economic pressure was applied by the sudden cancellation of lend-lease, while administration officials effectively frustrated Soviet hopes for financial aid in the form of German reparations or a large American loan (Kuklick, 1972). On the other hand, 'revisionists' noted that American assistance was liberally given to right-wing regimes in Greece and Turkey with the clear intention of establishing anti-communist governments on the very borders of the Soviet Union. One writer has even contended that Truman used the atomic bomb in 1945 not so much to defeat Japan as to terrify the Soviets into making concessions to the United States over Eastern Europe (Alperovitz, 1965). The thrust of these arguments is that Truman and his 'get tough' policy must bear a heavy responsibility for provoking the Cold War.

By concentrating on the importance of internal rather than external influences, the 'revisionists' found themselves obliged to explain the dynamics of American foreign policy. Influenced by the Vietnam War and more than two decades of huge defence spending, one scholar has stressed the primacy of the 'national security state'. According to this view, the well-established anti-Soviet prejudices of the State Department fused with the requirements of the military-industrial complex to propel the United States into what became a virtual war economy. The logical result was the state of Cold War with the Soviet Union (Yergin, 1978). The role of business and 'corporate' interests was particularly prominent in the the shaping and implementation of the Marshall Plan (Hogan, 1987).

A similar and very influential interpretation has stressed the significance of economic factors (Williams, 1962; Kolko and Kolko, 1972; LaFeber, 1976). These 'revisionist' or 'new left' historians have argued that American diplomacy has historically sought to serve the needs of American capitalism by seeking an 'open door' into overseas markets. In 1945 American officials were fearful of a recurrence of the Great Depression of the 1930s. They believed that American prosperity and even the survival of capitalism depended upon the creation of a liberal international economic order that would secure and guarantee the principle of the 'open door'. This aim clashed not so much with Soviet economic needs as with Stalin's security considerations. His desire for the protection provided by buffer states resulted in the creation of a Soviet 'closed' sphere of influence in Eastern Europe. The Truman administration sought to keep the region 'open' by exerting diplomatic and economic pressure. American economic expansionism compelled Stalin to consolidate his control over Eastern Europe and was therefore responsible for the Cold War.

Advocates of the 'orthodox' interpretation have complained that the 'revisionists' adopted double standards (Maddox, 1973). While Stalin was granted legitimate national security needs which excused his actions no matter how aggressive, the United States was judged according to an impossible standard of virtuous international behaviour. It was also pointed out that 'revisionists' have enjoyed the benefits of hindsight in formulating their arguments concerning the weakness of Soviet military forces. Although the Red Army was reduced in total strength after 1945, research has revealed that this was not apparent to American officials at the time. American military experts acknowledged that the Soviet Union was incapable of launching a direct military attack on the United States, but they also predicted that the Soviets could speedily overrun a weak and unstable Western Europe (Leffler, 1984, pp. 359–64). Moreover, this anxiety was not just an American preoccupation or fabrication. European leaders were also fearful of the Soviet threat. In his celebrated speech at Fulton, Missouri, in 1946 Churchill had sought to alert American public opinion to the creation of the 'Iron Curtain' in Europe. Indeed, the British Foreign Office considered that State Department officials were too passive towards the Soviet Union (Anderson, 1981; Hathaway, 1981).

There has also been considerable controversy over whether Truman actually initiated a sharp break in American policy. Despite his desire for conciliation and compromise, Roosevelt deliberately refrained from informing Stalin of the American development of the atomic bomb. Annoyed by Stalin's refusal to broaden the composition of the Polish government, Roosevelt told Churchill shortly before his death: 'We must not permit anybody to entertain a false impression that we are afraid. Our armies will in a very few days be in a position that will permit us to become "tougher" than has heretofore appeared advantageous to the war effort' (Dallek, 1979, p. 527). In contrast to his predecessor, Truman was inexperienced in foreign affairs and more receptive to the advice of anti-communist aides such as Ambassador Averell Harriman and Admiral William Leahy. Nevertheless, his decision to send his aide, Harry Hopkins, on a private mission to Moscow in May 1945 was reminiscent of Roosevelt's personal diplomacy and showed Truman's similar desire to seek agreement rather than confrontation with Stalin.

Furthermore, Truman was not simply an unwitting tool of military or business interests. The military-industrial complex had grown enormously during World War II, but its postwar ambitions were limited by political realities and the desire for demobilization within the United States itself. 'Atomic diplomacy' to coerce the Soviets was hardly feasible so long as the number of available atomic bombs was virtually nil (Sherwin, 1975). The Truman administration was certainly keen to promote exports and investment, but the devastated region of Eastern Europe was hardly a priority in this respect. In fact, the implementation of an alleged grand design to dominate the world economy was severely constrained by domestic politics. Congress even balked at granting a postwar loan to Britain, America's closest ally. Moreover, the Marshall Plan was carefully scrutinized by congressmen who were more concerned with its actual real costs than its possible future benefits.

Despite the claim made during the 1980s that a 'postrevisionist' synthesis has emerged among American historians, the historical controversy over the origins of the Cold War has continued and is in danger of going round in circles (Gaddis, 1983; Leffler, 1992, 1994). If there has been any common ground, it is the agreement that American policymakers were acutely suspicious of the intentions of the Soviet Union and irritated by its stubborn refusal to cooperate in making the postwar world over in the American image. The political vacuum in Central and Eastern Europe combined with the presence of large military forces made Europe the centre of diplomatic attention and the focus of superpower conflict. At this point historical interpretations diverge. 'Orthodox' writers argue that Stalin was bent on world conquest and had to be resisted. 'Revisionists' single out Truman as the instrument of economic forces and conclude that Stalin was a victim of unreasonable American pressure to concede a global 'open door'. The 'postrevisionists' contend that both leaders pursued pragmatic policies and should share responsibility for their mistakes and misperceptions that allowed the Cold War to take place. Stalin was cautious and averse to embarking upon another full-scale war in Europe, even though he was keen to extend Soviet borders at the expense of the West. While Truman was determined to resist communist aggression, his tough rhetoric disguised the lack of a coherent and systematic American strategy. As mentioned above, the governments of Western Europe, especially Britain, were perturbed by what they regarded as American indifference towards the military threat posed by the Soviet Union in Europe (Frazier, 1984). This has raised the question of the actions of other European powers and their particular contribution to the outbreak of the Cold War. For example, the evident success of Western European leaders in persuading the United States to become directly involved in European affairs has resulted in the interpretation that America acquired an 'empire by invitation' rather than by deliberate intention (Lundestad, 1990).

The role of countries remote from Europe has also become a

pertinent subject for research into the origins of the Cold War. The controversy over Iran in 1946 actually predated the Truman Doctrine and can be seen as the first test of strength between Truman and Stalin (Kuniholm, 1980). Similarly, reports of the activities of the communists in China and North Korea worried officials in the Truman administration and helped to confirm their suspicions of a monolithic communist conspiracy (Goncharov et al., 1993). The inclusion of events in Asia during the late 1940s in studies of the evolving Cold War between the United States and the Soviet Union points the way to a wider international perspective to the subject. Consequently, the communist victory in China in 1949 and the outbreak of the Korean War in 1950 do not appear as such sudden and inexplicable events.

No matter which person, country or system is held responsible or whether all were equally culpable, the historical fact is that the United States and the Soviet Union ended World War II as allies but had become adversaries by 1947. The confrontational relationship was notable in taking on the peculiar state of 'cold' war in which each side regularly heaped abuse upon the other and vigorously prepared for a 'hot' war that never actually materialized.

2

Stalemate in Europe

The Berlin Blockade

In direct accordance with American intentions, the Marshall Plan envisaged a significant stimulus to the economies of the three Western zones in Germany. The Soviets were apprehensive of future developments and accused the United States not only of selfishly seeking to monopolize the economic resources of the Ruhr but also of preparing for the creation of a separate West German political state. Fearful of the emergence of an anti-communist and unfriendly West Germany, the Soviets attempted to prevent this from happening by using the anomalous status of Berlin to make Germany the focus of international tension during 1948.

The ostensible basis of Soviet displeasure was their exclusion from Western deliberations on the political and economic future of Germany. Since the formation of Bizonia in 1947 the three Western powers had pursued a unilateral course. The Four-power Allied Control Council was ignored in 1948 as they discussed among themselves the incorporation of the French zone and the drafting of a new constitution to permit a measure of German self-government. Moreover, in order to integrate the Western zones more fully into the Marshall Plan, the three powers also announced their intention to replace the greatly depreciated Reichsmark with the new Deutsche Mark. Indeed, the issue of 'currency reform' highlighted the deterioration of relations between East and West. In retaliation for not being directly consulted, the Soviets formally withdrew from the Allied Control Council in March 1948. When the new currency was introduced into West Berlin in June, the Soviets declared that the Western powers had 'destroyed' the Four-power basis of governing Germany agreed at the Potsdam conference and had consequently forfeited 'the legal basis which assured their right to participate in the administration of Berlin' (Schlesinger, 1983, I, p. 483). On 24 June the Soviet authorities instituted a formal blockade by closing all road, rail and water routes to and from the city. Shortly afterward, the inhabitants of the Western sectors were cut off from all external supplies of fuel, power and food.

It was not surprising that Stalin should seek to make an issue over the city which Nikita Khrushchev later described as a bone in the Soviet throat. Smack in the middle of the Eastern zone, 'West Berlin' represented a symbolic Western presence. To many thousands of refugees seeking to flee the drab Eastern sector, the Western sector appeared as a magnetic island of freedom. But its geographical isolation was a decided weakness for the West. Outnumbered and surrounded by the Red Army, the small Western garrison of 7,500 troops was placed in an untenable military position. Moreover, the Western rights of access to their sectors of the city had never been precisely defined and were based on informal understandings made at the close of the war in 1945. The preponderance of military power clearly rested with the Soviet authorities, who could close the surface routes whenever they might wish to do so. West Berlin was therefore a hostage to Soviet whims or designs and frequently became the principle centre of Cold War tension in Europe.

The sudden and unexpected imposition of the blockade in June 1948 caused consternation in the West, where it was interpreted as calculated aggression by Stalin to force a humiliating Western withdrawal from Berlin prior to the extension of Soviet control over the whole city. However, instead of facing a direct Soviet military attack, the Western powers had to contend with a challenge that was primarily political and psychological in nature. While any attempt to break the blockade by force entailed the risk of unleashing a third world war, the alternative was to evacuate the garrison and thereby place two million West Berliners under Soviet rule. But withdrawal had little appeal for American officials, who considered that it would shatter Western prestige not only in Germany but all over Europe. Moreover, the suspicion existed that Stalin did not want war and that he was seeking a public relations triumph, to divert attention from his own current difficulties with the independently minded Josip Broz Tito in Yugoslavia and the recent failure of national strikes organized by communists in France and Italy. From his vantage point in Germany, General Clay advised a showdown. He was confident that the dispatch of an armed American convoy along the autobahn to Berlin would break the blockade and drive the Soviets into ignominious retreat: 'If we withdraw, our position in Europe is threatened. If America does not understand this now, does not know that the issue is cast, then it never will and communism will run rampant' (Clay, 1950, p. 361).

President Truman did not disagree. 'We are going to stay, period', he characteristically asserted (Millis, 1951, p. 454). But the fear of war ruled out Clay's recommendation to risk a military confrontation. The answer and salvation for the city and its inhabitants was found in airlifting supplies. In what was an extraordinary and unprecedented logistical achievement, thousands of tons of food and fuel were flown each day through narrow air corridors into the beleaguered city. The West was able to compensate for its military inadequacy on the ground by demonstrating its superiority in the air. Moreover, the Soviets were presented with the acute dilemma of whether or not to use force to halt the airlift in the knowledge that, by firing the first shot, they would incur responsibility for initiating hostilities.

Simultaneously, the Western authorities declared that the Soviet action was illegal and instituted a counter-blockade against the Eastern zone. More ominously, a number of American B-29 bombers capable of delivering atomic weapons at long range were moved from the United States to bases in Britain. The threat of the atomic bomb was never utilized because the Soviets were already effectively outmanoeuvred. Although they carefully avoided interfering with the airlift, the Soviet authorities still appeared in the eyes of world opinion as ruthlessly seeking to starve millions of men, women and children into submission. By contrast, the Western pilots were heroes and saviours.

On 12 May 1949 Stalin acknowledged defeat and reopened all routes into the city. The blockade had lasted 324 days, during which the West had airlifted more than two million tons of supplies. Although its legal right of access to Berlin still remained unclarified, the West claimed a victory in the first major confrontation of the superpowers in Europe. Far from undermining Western resolve, the blockade boosted morale and emphasized the close affinity of interests between Western Europe and the United States. The significance of airpower and resolute American leadership was abundantly vindicated. Furthermore, instead of preventing the formation of a West German state, the crisis over Berlin actually accelerated the process by substantially strengthening anti-communism throughout Western Europe and especially in West Germany. Although the United States, Britain and France would continue their military occupation, the granting of political independence in the three Western zones was signified in September 1949 by the establishment of the Federal Republic of Germany (FRG or West Germany). West Berlin was included in the new republic, but the decision to locate the capital 'provisionally' at Bonn underlined the importance attached to maintaining close links with the West. In October, Stalin responded by creating the German Democratic Republic (GDR or East Germany). The end of the zonal system had resulted not in reunification but in the division of Germany into two separate countries with opposed political systems and militarily aligned against each other.

Formation of NATO

Coming only a few months after a successful communist coup in Czechoslovakia, the Berlin crisis rekindled Western fears of communist aggression and directed attention to the urgent need for a Western military alliance. As early as March 1948 the governments of Britain, France, Belgium, Luxemburg and the Netherlands had signed the Brussels Pact to provide for mutual military assistance in the event of war. America's traditional aversion to entering into 'entangling alliances' with European powers meant, however, that the Truman administration remained aloof. Nevertheless, Truman welcomed the treaty in principle and was pleased to commend the development publicly. 'I am sure', he told Congress, 'that the determination of the free countries of Europe to protect themselves will be matched by an equal determination on our part to help them to do so' (Schlesinger, 1983, I, p. 128).

Rather than presidential statements of approval, the Western European governments wanted the formal commitment of American military power to defend Europe. Without the deterrent of American airpower and atomic weapons, they believed that there could be no real security against communist aggression. The supreme commander of the Brussels Pact forces, Field Marshal Bernard L. Montgomery, acknowledged that, in the event of war against the Soviets, he was supposed to maintain a defensive line along the Rhine. 'With present forces,' he lamented, 'I might be able to hold the tip of the Brittany Peninsula for 48 hours' (Achilles, 1985, p. 32). The Truman administration was sympathetic, but questioned whether Europe's defence required the United States to enter into a formal military alliance in peacetime. There were also formidable political obstacles to overcome. 'We shall be lucky if the President and the American Senatorial leaders pronounce in favour of a treaty binding the US for the first time in history to accept positive obligations in the way of defence of her natural associates and friends', noted the British foreign minister, Ernest Bevin, in April 1948 (Baylis, 1990, pp. 16-17).

The passage in June 1948 of the Vandenberg Resolution by a large majority of the American Senate indicated, however, the existence of considerable bipartisan political support in Congress for some form of American 'association' with the Brussels Pact. Congressmen were impressed by arguments stressing the natural affinities and common strategic interests between the two continents. They were receptive to the idea that the actual front line for the defence of democracy was not so much the Atlantic Ocean which separated America from Europe as the River Elbe which divided the two Germanies. The crisis over Berlin had also been timely and instructive in demonstrating the vital importance of American leadership to counter aggression. Moreover, administration officials became increasingly fearful that European insecurity threatened to undermine the work of the Marshall Plan. They considered that economic aid was not enough and that American military assistance was urgently required to enable the free nations of Europe to recover economically and politically. Otherwise, as Secretary of State Dean Acheson warned, they would 'succumb one by one to the erosive and encroaching processes of Soviet expansion' (Graebner, 1984, p. 149).

For much of 1948 the Western governments engaged in prolonged and complex discussions at Washington in an attempt to define the exact nature of America's commitment. As the result of a British suggestion, the area to be offered protection was enlarged to comprise not only the United States and the countries of the

Brussels Pact but also Canada, Scandinavia and the northern Mediterranean. The adoption of the term 'North Atlantic' secured American military participation and made the region more strategically viable. Moreover, by emphasizing the collective security aspect of the alliance it would also be more politically acceptable to the parliaments of the prospective member states.

A more difficult issue revolved around American doubts over the desirability of having an actual treaty. Despite the support for the Vandenberg Resolution, it was known that several senators, including Vandenberg himself, preferred their government to confine itself to giving a single, unilateral commitment similar to the Monroe Doctrine. Mindful of America's geographical position 3,000 miles away and its retreat into isolationism after World War I, the Western European governments argued that a formal treaty containing a binding guarantee was essential to underline the long-term intention of the United States to participate in the defence of Europe. 'France, on the outposts of Europe, cannot hold out alone', stated the French prime minister, Henri Queuille. He added: 'If sufficient forces could be relied on to prevent the Russian army from crossing the Elbe, the civilization of Europe would be safe. A fortnight after an invasion it would be lost' (Delmas, 1985, p. 64).

American officials recognized the need for a binding treaty rather than a loose association. But considerable discussion ensued before they eventually conceded the guarantee contained in article 5:

> The Parties agree that an armed attack against one or more of them in Europe or North America shall be considered an attack against them all; and . . . if such an armed attack occurs, each of them . . . will assist the Party or Parties so attacked by taking forthwith, individually and in concert with other Parties, such action as it deems necessary, including the use of armed force, to restore and maintain the security of the North Atlantic area.(Schlesinger, 1983, I, p. 141)

Despite the reference to collective action by all members, the ultimate effectiveness of the alliance depended upon the employment of American military power. Consequently, the deliberate mention of 'the use of armed force' in article 5 pleased the European governments. The United States, however, was careful to avoid giving an automatic commitment to go to war. According to the American Constitution only Congress could declare a state of war. American officials insisted therefore on the inclusion of article 11, which stated that implementation of the treaty must be in accordance with 'respective constitutional processes' (Schlesinger, 1983, I, p. 142). On 4 April 1949 the North Atlantic Treaty was signed in Washington by the United States, the five nations of the Brussels Pact, Canada, Denmark, Iceland, Italy, Portugal and Norway. Provision was made for regular meetings of the North Atlantic Council and the establishment of a permanent organization which would become known as NATO.

In July 1949 the American Senate ratified the treaty by a vote of 82 to 13. The debate revealed that Americans conceived of the alliance primarily as a psychological boost to a politically frightened and economically depressed Western Europe. In the immediate aftermath of Stalin's lifting of the Berlin blockade, there seemed no imminent likelihood of an all-out Soviet invasion of Western Europe. Initially, NATO could therefore develop a strategy which was relatively inexpensive. A concept which soon gained popularity was that of 'the shield and the sword'. Europe would provide the shield in the form of conventional ground forces to halt a Soviet attack while the sword was represented by the atomic weapons of America's Strategic Air Command (SAC). Moreover, the military burden was scarcely a crushing one for the United States. The atomic bomb served principally as a deterrent to the Soviet Union. It might never need to be used and would remain under independent American control. While two American divisions would continue to stay in Germany, there was no intention of dispatching additional American troops to replace European forces. As in the Marshall Plan, the Europeans were expected to assume the leading role in defending themselves.

This limited and defensive concept was rapidly altered by events. The discovery in August 1949 that the Soviets had successfully tested an atomic bomb dumbfounded American military experts, who had not expected such a development for at least another ten years. 'This is now a different world', remarked Senator Vandenberg (Cook, 1989, p. 229). Furthermore, the passing of the American monopoly on atomic weapons coincided with communist success in seizing control of mainland China. The mood of anxiety prevailing in Washington was reflected in a comprehensive review of America's armed forces undertaken on behalf of the National Security Council. Known as NSC-68, the secret report was completed in April 1950. Starting with the premise that the Soviet Union still actively sought world domination, NSC-68 argued that the military power of the United States was currently inadequate to prevent this. The report concluded that the United States must undertake an enormous military effort on a scale commensurate with wartime rearmament. It was considered unlikely, however, that Congress would readily agree to a massive increase in the annual defence budget. But the timing of NSC-68 was fortuitous. The sudden outbreak of the Korean War in June 1950 appeared to confirm the report's findings. The United States was plunged into a war on behalf of the United Nations against what appeared to be undeniable, naked communist aggression. The anticipated congressional opposition to NSC-68 was subdued and large defence appropriations were quickly secured. 'Korea came along and saved us', Secretary of State Acheson later admitted (LaFeber, 1976, p. 100).

The invasion of South Korea had direct relevance for Europe since it raised the spectre of a similar communist attack against West Germany. The threat was made even more acute by the loss of America's atomic monopoly and the alarming imbalance in conventional forces between West and East. While the NATO countries could put up to 14 divisions into the field in Europe, the Soviets were believed to possess at least 125. Imbued with a sense of crisis mixed with the crusading spirit inherent in NSC-68, American policymakers considered that it was imperative to build up NATO's ground forces. But disharmony soon appeared within the alliance. The European governments lacked the economic resources of the United States. They were reluctant to rearm in peacetime and thereby damage their plans for much-needed economic revival. There was also awareness that the burden of building up costly and politically unpopular conventional forces was meant to fall primarily upon them rather than the United States. Furthermore, a move towards rearmament contained the risk of alarming the Soviets and provoking them to launch a pre-emptive invasion.

In 1949 the United States had insisted on a North Atlantic treaty that was inherently flexible and left a wide latitude for future manoeuvre. A year later, in order to secure European agreement to rearm, the United States made its commitment to NATO more tangible and permanent. Acting to all intents and purposes like a European power, the United States now assumed the central military command of NATO's ground forces and promised to place additional troops in Europe. As a demonstration of the sincerity of

American intentions General Eisenhower, who had commanded American forces in Europe during World War II and was well known and very popular among Western European leaders, was appointed Supreme Allied Commander Europe (SACEUR). From his headquarters in Paris he headed a unified command structure composed of forces representing all the member states. The protection of each and every ally was affirmed by the adoption of a 'forward strategy' that aimed at defending Europe as far to the east as possible.

The new strategy raised, however, the question of defending West Germany. The formation of the Federal Republic of Germany in 1949 had been very much at America's instigation and was intended not only to gain a friend for the West but also to establish a buffer against Soviet expansion. Nevertheless, while NATO included West Germany within its defensive plans, that country was not a member of the alliance and made no contribution to its own defence. The logic of incorporating German troops within NATO was conclusively accepted by the Truman administration, but Acheson's suggestion of raising ten German divisions in September 1950 only disconcerted the European allies. Embittered by the memory of three German invasions in less than a century, France was terrified at the prospect of a rearmed Germany. The French government grudgingly agreed to the principle of West German military participation in NATO only after the United States undertook to increase military aid and to integrate American troops fully within NATO's command structure. In this way the Western European allies were partially compensated for bearing the heavy costs of rearmament and given a guarantee of American protection against an invader whether from the Soviet Union or from Germany. In effect, the United States was adopting a policy of 'double containment'. A contemporary quip was that NATO had been created to keep the Germans down, the Americans in and the Russians out.

In January 1951 General Eisenhower returned to Europe intent upon ensuring 'the survival of Western civilization' (Ambrose, 1983b, p. 496). He expressed confidence that the current disparity in conventional forces between West and East would soon be redressed. Support was forthcoming from the members of NATO, who all pledged substantial increases in defence spending. The American Congress also agreed to send four extra divisions to Germany. Britain announced that it would retain military conscription. But a discordant note was sounded by George Kennan, who had once warned of the danger 'of a general preoccupation with military affairs, to the detriment of economic recovery and of the necessity for seeking a peaceful solution to Europe's difficulties' (Kennan, 1968, p. 410). His fears were fulfilled as the acceleration of the arms race between the superpowers resulted in an intensification of the Cold War.

Rearmament

'The North Atlantic pact', declared the Soviet Union in March 1949, 'is designed to daunt the states which do not agree to obey the dictates of the Anglo-American grouping of powers that lay claim to world domination' (Schlesinger, 1983, II, p. 404). The prospect of further hostile military encirclement merely motivated Stalin to increase the strength of the Red Army from 2.8 million in 1948 to 5 million in 1953. Additional resources were directed into weapons programmes that would ultimately lead to Soviet development of atomic and hydrogen bombs. Moreover, the spectre of German rearmament and West Germany's formal incorporation within NATO presented the Soviet leaders with an extremely useful propaganda tool to justify and call for continued sacrifices from their own people and those of the countries of Eastern Europe.

Behind what was referred to in the West as 'the Iron Curtain', a Soviet empire of satellite states stretched from the Baltic to the Balkans. Although they nominally retained their independent identities and were members of the United Nations, these countries were carefully subordinated to Soviet political, economic and military direction. Obedience was ensured by the presence or the close proximity of the Red Army. Any tendency towards political dissent was ruthlessly eliminated so that no repetition of Yugoslavia's defection in 1948 was allowed. Economic controls were imposed in 1949 by the creation of the Council for Mutual Economic Assistance (Comecon or CMEA), which provided an alternative to the Marshall Plan. Military affairs were also firmly under Soviet command. Training, the allocation of resources and military planning were coordinated from Moscow. A Soviet counterpart of NATO was therefore soon in existence although the establishment of the formal military alliance known as the Warsaw

Treaty Organization (WTO or Warsaw Pact) was not publicly announced until May 1955.

In the United States, the desire to liberate Eastern Europe from communist tyranny became a prominent theme of Eisenhower's presidential election campaign of 1952. The leading Republican authority on foreign affairs, John Foster Dulles, denounced the Truman administration for acting passively and declared that the United States must seize the initiative in the Cold War. Dulles fervently preached an 'end of the negative, futile and immoral policy of "containment" which abandons countless human beings to a despotism and Godless terrorism' (Halle, 1967, p. 270). The increasingly moralistic and uncompromising tone of Dulles towards the Soviet Union reflected not only the strategic imperatives of NSC-68 but also the prevailing American mood of virtual paranoia associated with McCarthyism, the 'loss' of China and the Korean War. The perception of communism as an evil that must be extirpated had a powerful political appeal and contributed significantly to the election of Eisenhower in November 1952.

Eisenhower's victory led to the appointment of Dulles as secretary of state. Despite his tough campaign rhetoric, Dulles proved more circumspect in office. Nevertheless, 'rolling back' the Iron Curtain in Europe was still declared to be a priority. This would be achieved, however, not by military force but by steadily exerting the superior moral and spiritual example of the 'free world' under the leadership of the United States. A 'war of words' was conducted in which Dulles claimed to speak from an unassailable position of strength. In his opinion, America was the most powerful economic country in the world and its generous aid in the form of the Marshall Plan had stimulated the beginning of what was to become an economic miracle in Western Europe. This was evident in the marked contrast between the prosperous societies of Western Europe and the drab and impoverished people of the East. Further evidence of the triumph of democracy was the political decline of communist parties throughout the West. Communist rule was thoroughly discredited by its identification with purges, show trials, labour camps and immense suffering. 'We know', Dulles stated, 'that the Soviet Communists' attempts to impose their absolute rule over 800 million captives involves them in what, in the long run, is an impossible task' (Gaddis, 1982, pp. 155–6).

Despite its wish for bold action against the Soviets, the priority of the new Republican administration was to achieve a sound domestic economy and a balanced budget. 'Our problem', observed Eisenhower, 'is to achieve military strength within the limits of endurable strain upon our economy' (Graebner, 1984, p. 194). Truman's policy of containment by massive rearmament was therefore discarded because the escalating financial burden would ultimately have resulted in national bankruptcy. Instead, a strategy known as the 'New Look' emerged which allowed a significant reduction of expensive conventional forces by placing increased emphasis on strategic airpower. While the air force would be allowed to recruit an additional 30,000 men, the army would be reduced by 500,000. Nevertheless, America's destructive capacity would actually be enhanced by the acquisition of new airplanes and weapons systems giving 'more bang for the buck' (Divine, 1981, p. 37).

The 'New Look' policy aroused apprehension in Western Europe that the United States was contemplating a return to isolationism. So close had been his military association with Europe over many years that Eisenhower expressed himself 'amazed' at this reaction (Ambrose, 1984, p. 33). In his opinion, NATO remained the key to America's defence. In 1952 the alliance had been extended to cover the eastern Mediterranean by the adhesion of Greece and Turkey. At the Lisbon council meeting of NATO in 1952 a goal of 96 divisions was set for 1954. The Eisenhower administration was particularly keen to see the European allies build up their ground forces in order to compensate for the proposed reduction in similar American forces. The target set at Lisbon was, however, so ambitious that its achievement would inevitably require the inclusion of substantial West German forces.

After the shock that had initially greeted Acheson's proposal in 1950 of creating a German army, the Western European governments gradually became reconciled to the compelling military need for German rearmament. The main fear, especially in France, was the revival of Germany as an independent military power. Signs of Franco-German *rapprochement* were indicated, however, by the inclusion of the German Federal Republic in the European Coal and Steel Community (ECSC) formed in 1951. At the instigation of the French government, a scheme was devised to create a multinational Western European army under NATO's command to which German units would be assigned. This integrated army was modelled on the ECSC and was called the European Defence Community (EDC). A treaty to create the EDC was drawn up in 1952, but ratification encountered considerable resistance, particularly in the French National Assembly. Military experts questioned the feasibility of organizing an all-European army with a common uniform but different languages. Politicians argued that the concept encroached too far on national sovereignty.

When he had served as supreme allied commander of NATO, Eisenhower had constantly preached strength through unity. Ideally, he wished for a 'United States of Europe', which he believed would 'instantly . . . solve the real and bitter problems of today' (Ambrose, 1983a, p. 508). Consequently, the Eisenhower administration was strongly in favour of the EDC, seeing it as the best possible spur towards the political unification of Western Europe. Dismayed by the protracted political debate in France, Dulles warned that rejection of the treaty would compel an 'agonizing reappraisal' of American policy towards Western Europe and the likelihood of a separate arrangement between the United States and West Germany (Graebner, 1984, p. 192).

Dulles's intervention, however, proved counter-productive. Already resentful of American criticism of its colonial policies in Algeria and Indochina, the French government was eager to demonstrate publicly that France was not a satellite of the United States. Consequently, French rejection of the EDC in August 1954 threw American diplomacy into disarray. But the need for German military integration within NATO was not in question, so ways were sought to resolve the apparent impasse. The atmosphere of gloom was lifted in October by the acceptance of a British initiative to include West Germany in an enlargement of the Brussels Treaty to be known as the Western European Union (WEU). Britain also announced that it would undertake to place four additional army divisions in Germany. These moves gave the political and military reassurances required by the French government and paved the way for the acceptance of West Germany as a full member of NATO in 1955. In return for recognition as an independent sovereign nation, West Germany agreed to restrict the size of its armed forces and undertook not to manufacture nuclear weapons, long-range missiles or bombers.

The defeat of the EDC coincided with a slackening of defence spending by the NATO countries. Europeans were just as reluctant as American taxpayers to see high military expenditures undermine their hopes of sustained economic growth. Rearmament was politically unpopular and held responsible for inflation and balance of payments difficulties. Countries such as Britain and France also found it impossible to give a priority to NATO when they faced pressing military commitments in their overseas colonial empires. Moreover, as the crises over the Berlin blockade and the outbreak of the Korean War receded into the past, there was less fear in Europe of imminent Soviet invasion.

The successful testing of the hydrogen bomb in 1952 and later deployment of tactical nuclear weapons also brought into question the rationale for maintaining large standing armies. NATO's goal of 96 divisions proved excessively optimistic and was quickly reduced to 43. By 1954 only 25 divisions could be described as combat ready. Even with German rearmament, it was clear that NATO's ground forces were inadequate to defend Europe from a full-scale Soviet attack. They could only hope to slow the aggressor's advance and thereby give time for the use of American strategic airpower. Western Europe's tacit reliance upon the latter had existed virtually since 1945, but Dulles gave it the new name of the strategy of 'massive retaliation'. 'We cannot build', he declared, 'a 20,000 mile Maginot Line or match the Red armies, man for man, gun for gun and tank for tank at any particular time or place their general staff selected' (Gaddis, 1982, p. 121). Instead, Dulles argued, the United States must use the 'deterrent of massive retaliatory power' and 'respond vigorously at places and with means of its own choosing' (Schlesinger, 1983, I, p. 230).

The European allies appreciated the advantages of substituting technology for conventional forces, but they were alarmed by the implications of 'massive retaliation'. They feared that the United States might transform a minor local conflict into a world war or, conversely, choose to back down in a crisis rather than precipitate nuclear devastation. To insure against the latter contingency taking place on their own continent, they insisted that American troops remain in Germany as a visible guarantee of America's binding commitment to the defence of Europe. This function was described as a 'trip wire' or 'plate glass window'. Moreover, even if NATO's troops were unable to defend Europe against a full-scale Soviet invasion, they must still be seen to possess a credible capacity to deter aggression. Consequently, it was decided in 1954 to compensate for the lack of conventional forces by deploying tactical nuclear weapons under American command. The use of low-yield nuclear weapons would, however, be strictly restricted to the immediate battle zone. 'We have determined that our strategy in the center requires the use of atomic weapons, whether the enemy uses them or not', stated General Alfred M. Gruenther in 1954. The supreme allied commander added: 'We must use atomic bombs to redress the imbalance between their forces and ours to achieve victory' (Osgood, 1962, p. 109). Technological advance brought tangible economic benefits, but it also introduced a balance of terror in which war posed the appalling prospect of annihilation.

If the threat of nuclear holocaust deterred a Soviet invasion of Western Europe, it also effectively prevented the United States from 'rolling back' the Iron Curtain. Despite Soviet political weakness after the death of Stalin in 1953, the new leaders of the Kremlin were determined to maintain control over Eastern Europe. Disturbances in East Germany in 1953 and Poland in 1956 were quickly quelled. When a major revolt occurred in Hungary in 1956, it was ruthlessly suppressed by Soviet tanks. Dulles praised the patriotism of the rebels and led the condemnation of Soviet brutality at the United Nations. But his attitude of moral superiority rang hollow as Soviet tanks and troops patrolled the streets of Budapest. Eisenhower privately admitted that the use of atomic weapons had been suggested in discussions about possible American intervention. 'But to annihilate Hungary', he despairingly concluded, 'is in no way to help her' (Ambrose, 1984, p. 372). Despite the stress on rearmament and acquiring a position of military strength, the Eisenhower administration was unwilling to intervene militarily. In effect, the United States tacitly acknowledged that Eastern Europe was a Soviet sphere of influence.

Decline of the Cold War in Europe

While the Soviets remained impervious to American criticism of their stranglehold over Eastern Europe, a more amenable diplomatic approach towards the West was evident in other matters. The death of Stalin in March 1953 afforded an opportunity to ease tensions. 'We are not angry with anybody', stressed the new Soviet leader, Georgi Malenkov (Ulam, 1973, p. 208). Churchill suggested an immediate 'summit' meeting, but Dulles was highly suspicious of Malenkov's 'phony peace campaign' (Divine, 1981, p. 109). The chance of *détente* was therefore lost. Nevertheless, aggressive actions such as the blockade of Berlin were not repeated. Instead, Soviet diplomatic influence was exerted to assist in bringing about a cease-fire in Korea in 1953. Proposals also emanated from Moscow for a Four-power agreement to end the military occupation of Germany by creating a unified and neutral country. Although the German question remained unresolved a similar scheme was acceptable in the case of Austria, which had also been under Four-power control and administration since 1945. Indeed, the signing of the Austrian Treaty in 1955 raised hopes of a 'thaw' in the Cold War and enabled President Eisenhower to propose a summit meeting to 'change the spirit' of relations between the superpowers (Ambrose, 1984, p. 261).

For the first time since the Potsdam conference exactly ten years earlier, the leaders of the great powers met together at Geneva in July 1955. The agenda covered many subjects ranging from disarmament to Germany. The talks, however, were inconclusive and the powers simply agreed to disagree. 'They drank little and smiled much', was how Eisenhower summed up the behaviour of the Soviet leaders, Nicolai Bulganin and Nikita Khrushchev (Divine, 1981, p. 119). The president also mentioned that each side 'intended to pursue a new spirit of conciliation and cooperation in its contacts with the other' (Ambrose, 1984, p. 267). This optimism was, however, sorely tested by the brutal Soviet suppression of the Hungarian uprising during 1956.

Emboldened by the West's passivity during the Hungarian crisis, Soviet diplomacy subsequently assumed a more aggressive and challenging tone which contrasted sharply with the defensive mentality shown during the Stalin era. Indeed, the West faced a formidable antagonist in Khrushchev, who finally achieved political supremacy over his rivals and became general secretary in 1957. At the Twentieth Communist Party Congress in 1956, Khrushchev had denounced the excesses and errors caused by Stalin's 'cult of personality'. The speech created shock waves throughout the communist bloc, but it achieved its purpose of giving an impetus and enhanced respectability to international communism. The ideological fervour of the new Soviet leader did not go unheeded in the West, for Khrushchev represented a nation which now possessed its own growing arsenal of nuclear weapons. Moreover, in October 1957 the Soviet Union delivered an enormous psychological blow to American pride by sending an artificial satellite, the 'sputnik', around the earth. By fitting a warhead to the rocket that launched the satellite, a new weapon was produced which was faster and less vulnerable than the bomber. The age of the intercontinental ballistic missile (ICBM) was thereby inaugurated and the initial advantage lay with the Soviet Union. However, in what he saw as the intensification of the struggle for 'peaceful coexistence' between capitalism and communism, Khrushchev asserted that the economic and scientific progress of communist countries would defeat the West without any need to resort to war. He explained in 1956: 'The mighty camp of socialism, with its population of over 900,000,000, is growing and gaining in strength. Its huge internal forces, its decisive advantages over capitalism are being increasingly revealed from day to day' (Schlesinger, 1983, II, p. 549). At the Twenty-second Communist Party Congress in 1961 Khrushchev even predicted that the standard of living of the Soviet people would overtake that of the United States within twenty years.

Meanwhile a significant test of strength had occurred in Berlin. Khrushchev's boasts about the superiority of the communist system and way of life rang hollow in the city where the western sectors had visibly enjoyed growing economic property since 1949 while the eastern sector languished. During the ensuing decade almost two million East German refugees travelled to Berlin in order to escape to the West. Suddenly in November 1958, Khrushchev created an international crisis by demanding an end to what he called the use of West Berlin as 'a springboard for intensive espionage, sabotage, and other subversive activities' (Schlesinger, 1983, II, p. 603). Although he did not impose a military blockade as Stalin had done ten years earlier, Khrushchev adopted the same tactics of political and psychological warfare. If the Western garrisons were not withdrawn from the city within six months, the Soviets threatened to sign a separate peace treaty with the government of East Germany which would place all the access routes under the latter's control. Such an outcome would be unacceptable to the Western powers since they did not recognize East Germany as an independent nation. To ignore Khrushchev's ultimatum, however, would entail the risk of provoking a military confrontation which might result in nuclear war.

Eisenhower regarded Khrushchev's action as part of a calculated Soviet strategy to probe the West's most vulnerable spots. 'They would like us to go frantic every time they stir up difficulties in these areas', he noted (Ambrose, 1984, p. 520). Nevertheless, the president believed that the United States had a 'solemn obligation' to defend the citizens of West Berlin (Divine, 1981, p. 33). Although he was determined to stand firm, Eisenhower wished to avoid war. Subsequent diplomatic events demonstrated that Khrushchev also sought conciliation rather than confrontation. When the British prime minister, Harold Macmillan, visited Moscow in March 1959 he was told that the Soviets would call off the deadline if a summit meeting was arranged. Eisenhower countered by insisting that a preliminary meeting of foreign ministers must be held first at Geneva. Khrushchev agreed and quietly abandoned the original deadline. The foreign ministers met at Geneva in May and Khrushchev later visited the United States in September. A summit meeting was eventually held at Paris in May 1960, but any chance of substantive discussions was rendered abortive by the shooting down of a U-2 American reconnaissance spy-plane over the Soviet Union.

Thwarted over Berlin, Khrushchev used Eisenhower's belated admission of having had prior knowledge of the U-2 spy flights as a propaganda club with which to humiliate the United States. The Soviet defence minister, Marshal Rodion Malinovsky, ominously warned that his country possessed the weapons to strike 'both at the satellites and at the leader' of the western alliance, 'no matter what seas and oceans they may hide behind' (Halle, 1967, p. 375). But Soviet aggressiveness only gave further alarm to the West and stimulated another round of the arms race. Since the launch of the sputnik in 1957 some American military experts had claimed that the Soviets enjoyed such a decisive superiority in missile technology that they would soon be able to launch a devastating 'first strike' upon the United States. This fear was successfully exploited in the 1960 presidential election campaign by the Democratic candidate, John F. Kennedy, who charged that the ineptitude of the Eisenhower administration had allowed the creation of a 'missile gap' between the United States and the Soviet Union. On assuming the presidency in 1961, Kennedy signalled his intentions by requesting Congress to increase annual defence spending by an extra $6 billion.

The new president also sought a personal meeting with Khrushchev.

This took place at Vienna in June 1961. Prior to the summit, in April, Kennedy had experienced a humiliating set-back when a covert operation organized by the CIA had failed to overthrow Fidel Castro in Cuba. The American-sponsored army of Cuban exiles had been defeated and captured at the Bay of Pigs. At Vienna Khrushchev adopted a characteristically confident and forceful attitude. He tried to bully the younger man and renewed the Berlin crisis by again threatening to sign a peace treaty with East Germany. As the two leaders parted, Kennedy said: 'It's going to be a cold winter' (Salinger, 1967, p. 182). Some weeks later, Kennedy stated on national television that West Berlin 'has now become, as never before, the great testing place of Western courage and will'. Simultaneously, the president announced his decision to call up 150,000 army reservists and to increase the size of NATO's ground forces. Kennedy warned: 'We cannot and will not permit the Communists to drive us out of Berlin, either gradually or by force' (Schlesinger, 1983, I, p. 665).

In West Berlin, each day saw the arrival of more than one thousand East German refugees. Quite unexpectedly, the East German authorities erected a barbed-wire fence during the night of 12-13 August 1961. The fence soon became the notorious Berlin 'Wall' separating the Eastern and Western sectors. The 'Wall' was built up to a height of 20 feet and eventually extended to more than 25 miles in length. The West seized its opportunity to condemn a society that had to build a wall to keep its own people captive. The Soviets countered by describing West Berlin as a den of 'international criminals and provocateurs of all kinds' (Schlesinger, 1983, I, p. 672). The diplomatic dialogue was heated. 'The source of world trouble and tension is Moscow, not Berlin', declared Kennedy, and he added: 'And if war begins, it will have begun in Moscow and not Berlin' (Schlesinger, 1983, I, p. 666). But there was no disposition to resort to force. The Berlin crisis was allowed to fade away as both sides acknowledged that the partition of Germany was an undeniable fact. The Wall therefore achieved Khrushchev's purpose of halting the flood of refugees and gave valuable breathing space to the communist rulers of East Germany. On the other hand, West Germany was confirmed as a fully integrated member of the Western alliance. Moreover, Kennedy was given the opportunity to display qualities of firmness and leadership that compared favourably to Khrushchev's combination of bluff and bluster.

The balance of nuclear weaponry was also swinging decisively against the Soviet Union. There was, in fact, no missile gap. Even before Kennedy took office, the United States had made rapid strides in developing ICBMs including missiles that could be launched from Polaris submarines. American superiority in strategic weapons was further underlined in 1962 by the deployment of Titan and Minuteman land-based missiles. The United States appeared to have a 'first strike' capability and was forging even further ahead. Khrushchev secretly attempted to redress the strategic balance by placing nuclear missiles in Cuba. The Soviet leader later claimed that his action was 'defensive' and intended purely to protect Cuba from an imminent American invasion. Indeed, despite the failure of the Bay of Pigs operation, the Kennedy administration was continuing its efforts to 'destabilize' the Cuban revolutionary regime in what was known as 'Operation Mongoose'. But covert acts of sabotage in Cuba hardly required the emplacement of nuclear missiles. In fact, Khrushchev's resort to secrecy and deception conveyed the impression that the missiles were really intended to be 'offensive' weapons. Once installed, they would provide the Soviets with the means to threaten the destruction of the principal cities along the eastern seaboard of the United States.

In October 1962 American U-2 reconnaissance flights revealed that missile sites were under construction in Cuba. A shocked Kennedy hastily convened his advisers, who formed an Executive Committee (Ex Comm) of the National Security Council. Ex Comm remained in secret session throughout the 'Thirteen Days' of crisis. The president was determined to avoid a show of weakness, but he was fearful of starting off a nuclear war. Opinion was divided among his advisers. Some recommended air strikes or a military invasion to destroy the missile bases, while others advocated a diplomatic solution. It was believed, however, that the sites were not yet operational and that most of the Soviet military equipment was still at sea en route to Cuba. Kennedy therefore favoured the establishment of an American 'quarantine' or naval blockade of Cuba to prevent this equipment from reaching its destination. It was a calculated decision that indicated American firmness and also astutely allowed Khrushchev time to consider his reply.

On 22 October Kennedy appeared on television to inform the American people and the world of Khrushchev's 'clandestine, reckless and provocative threat to world peace' (Schlesinger, 1983,

III, p. 595). A sombre mood prevailed at the White House in Washington where American officials were worried that the Soviets might attempt to break through the naval blockade or create a diversion over Berlin. The world was poised on the edge of nuclear disaster as the two superpowers engaged in what Secretary of State Dean Rusk graphically described as an 'eyeball-to-eyeball' confrontation (Beschloss, 1991, p. 498). On 28 October Khrushchev 'blinked' and sent a telegram agreeing to dismantle the bases. Soviet ships en route to Cuba were turned around.

On the surface it seemed that Kennedy had achieved a famous diplomatic victory in forcing Khrushchev to climb down. Indeed, the accusation that he had given in to American nuclear blackmail was damaging to Khrushchev's authority in the Kremlin and contributed to his overthrow in 1964. During the actual 1962 crisis, however, President Kennedy showed no desire. to gloat or to humiliate the Soviet leader. He tactfully welcomed Khrushchev's telegram of 28 October and described it as 'an important contribution to peace' (Schlesinger, 1983, III, p. 606). In fact, Kennedy's diplomatic language reflected a secret compromise in which he had given Khrushchev an assurance that the United States would not invade Cuba. The president also undertook to withdraw obsolete American Jupiter missiles based in Turkey. Khrushchev was satisfied with what he regarded as 'psychological equality' with the United States (Lebow and Stein, 1994, p. 141).

Cuba was the country most directly affected by the Cuban Missile Crisis. While Kennedy had forced the removal of the Soviet missile sites, he had also deprived himself and his successors of the military option to invade the island and overthrow Fidel Castro. But the Missile Crisis had involved much more than the present or future condition of Cuba. The world had been taken to the very brink of nuclear war. It was an experience that chastened both Kennedy and Khrushchev. The desire to avoid a similar confrontation in the future was exemplified by Kennedy in a celebrated speech delivered at American University in June 1963. He stated:

> Let us examine our attitude toward the Cold War, remembering that we are not engaged in a debate, seeking to pile up debating points. We are not here distributing blame or pointing the finger of judgment. We must deal with the world as it is, and not as it might have been had the history of the last eighteen years been different. (Walton, 1973, p. 151)

Khrushchev later complimented Kennedy on 'the greatest speech by an American President since Roosevelt' (Schlesinger, 1965, p. 772). Symbolic of the changed mood was the setting up in 1963 of a direct 'hot line' for instant teletype communication between the Kremlin and the White House. After years of fruitless discussion, agreement was also rapidly reached in July 1963 on a Nuclear Test Ban Treaty to outlaw atmospheric tests. 'While it will not end the threat of nuclear war,' Kennedy noted that the treaty 'can reduce tensions, open a way to further agreements, and thereby help to ease the threat of war' (Schlesinger, 1983, II, p. 731).

The European members of NATO reacted ambivalently to the signs of improved relations between the superpowers. The development of massive Soviet nuclear forces during the 1950s had only made Western Europe even more dependent on the American nuclear deterrent. Far from increasing security, the result was a greater feeling of insecurity. Notably, President Charles de Gaulle of France argued that the defence of Europe had become a secondary consideration for the United States. Since America was now also in danger of a direct attack from long-range Soviet missiles, he questioned whether the United States would risk a nuclear exchange that might result in its own national extinction. With somewhat inverted logic, de Gaulle also contended that the United States was unreliable and a threat to world peace. Citing the example of the Cuban Missile Crisis, he claimed that Kennedy had been prepared to precipitate a nuclear war without consulting his allies in NATO. Consequently, de Gaulle sought an independent nuclear force for France and pointedly refused to join the Test Ban Treaty.

The French president's independent stance reflected not only his strong personality, but also the re-emergence of European prestige and influence. Since the dark days of the late 1940s, Western Europe had achieved spectacular economic growth and political stability. Under the impetus of the European Economic Community (EEC or Common Market), established in 1955 and formally constituted by the Treaty of Rome two years later, Western Europe was fast acquiring a new sense of common identity and self-esteem. In a striking reversal of historic tradition, Britain applied for admission to the EEC in 1962. But de Gaulle vetoed British membership. In his opinion, the application was part of a plot to extend America's control of NATO to the EEC. A mood of anti-Americanism was evident throughout Western Europe during the 1960s, but no government was willing to imitate de Gaulle's example of 1966 and withdraw their forces assigned to NATO. Nevertheless, while the countries of Western Europe continued to regard NATO as fundamental to their security, they were no longer so terrified of a Soviet invasion and wished to improve relations with the countries of the Eastern bloc.

Accustomed to unquestioned predominance in NATO, American officials were understandably surprised, if not irritated, by Europe's desire and capacity to assert its independence of action. Both Kennedy and his successor, Lyndon Johnson, were eager that the European allies should concentrate on building up their conventional forces. They contended that those governments were content to shelter under America's nuclear umbrella while doing too little to protect themselves. The argument was familiar, but the imperatives for action had changed by the beginning of the 1960s. More than a decade of peace and prosperity had bolstered Western Europe's self-confidence and sense of security. Despite the presence of enormous military forces facing each other in Central Europe, the prospect of mutual assured destruction (MAD) made war increasingly 'unthinkable'. Moreover, the frightening spectre of a monolithic communist conspiracy had been removed by the revelation of the existence of a serious split between the Soviet Union and China. The Cold War was hardly at an end, but Europeans regarded it as in decline. Indeed, as de Gaulle argued, the focal point of the struggle had demonstrably moved from Europe to Asia. While the images and language of the Cold War originated from the conflict between West and East over postwar Europe, the real military battles were actually taking place elsewhere in the world.

3

Conflict in Asia

The China Tangle

For more than a thousand years the vast Chinese empire exercised dominion over the countries of the Far East. However, during the nineteenth century, China's superior status was rudely challenged and diminished by the incursions of European powers. The 1911 revolution brought an end to the Chinese empire, but the new republic failed to achieve political and economic stability. Preoccupied with their own internal affairs, the nations of Europe were unable to exploit China's weakness. Consequently, Japan was the main beneficiary. Dating from its victory over tsarist Russia in 1904–5, Japan had steadily extended its influence and possessions on the Asian mainland. Japan's attack on Manchuria in 1931 widened six years later into full-scale war with China and was part of an ambitious strategy designed to establish the 'Greater East Asia Co-Prosperity Sphere'. But Japanese dreams of regional hegemony eventually provoked the direct military intervention of the United States.

Although American ties were historically closer to Europe than to the Far East, the United States also bordered the Pacific Ocean and consequently looked westwards to Asia. Its emerging commercial and strategic interests in this region were underlined by the acquisition of the Hawaiian and Philippine Islands in 1898–9. The United States also developed a particularly friendly relationship with China. A policy known as the 'open door' was pursued, in which American merchants gained equal access to the vast China market in return for their government's pledge to give diplomatic support for China's claims to territorial integrity and political independence. Within the United States, a 'China lobby' emerged to advocate closer political and economic links. Indeed, the American public needed little persuasion, for it manifested a genuine sympathy for the Chinese people in their struggle against European and Japanese imperialism. However, the desire to act as the self-appointed protector of China inevitably resulted in strained relations between the United States and Japan, culminating in the latter's pre-emptive assault on Pearl Harbor in 1941.

Despite the public demand for quick and massive military retaliation against Japan, the Roosevelt administration insisted on following a Europe-first strategy during World War II. American troops were sent to fight in Europe, but not on the Asian mainland. Instead, the United States preferred to mobilize its enormous air and naval power in a gradual island-hopping campaign across the Pacific. But Japanese resistance was fierce and fanatical. Consequently, the maintenance of a second military front in China became an important element of Roosevelt's Far Eastern strategy. American financial and military support was given to the nationalist government of Chiang Kai-shek (Jiang Jieshi) so that it could continue the war and thereby tie down large numbers of Japanese forces on the mainland. For the same reason, Roosevelt was eager to persuade Stalin to enter the war against Japan in August 1945.

Instead of a massive invasion of the Japanese home islands, the dropping of the atomic bombs in August 1945 brought an unexpectedly sudden Japanese surrender. Japan's defeat was total and confirmed that the United States was indisputably the predominant power in the region. A Four-power Allied Council consisting of the United States, the British Commonwealth, China and the Soviet Union was established at Tokyo. President Truman insisted, however, that the council exercise only an advisory function. In contrast to the situation in Europe, Japan was not allowed to become a contentious issue like Germany. Indeed, the United States pointedly refused to allow the Soviets to participate in the military occupation of Japan. The post of supreme commander was assigned to General Douglas MacArthur. With characteristic American idealism, MacArthur declared his intention to convert Japan into 'the world's greatest laboratory for an experiment in the liberation of a people from totalitarian military rule and for the liberalization of government from within' (Manchester, 1979, pp. 429–30). Soviet protests went unheeded as MacArthur proceeded to exercise autocratic control over a defeated nation which was to be disarmed and reformed according to American dictates.

Despite the controversy surrounding MacArthur's style of governing Japan, American diplomats were more interested in the postwar future of China. 'Americans', remarked George Kennan, 'tended to exaggerate China's real importance and to underrate that of Japan' (Kennan, 1968, p. 374). By restraining Japan, American diplomacy sought to alter the balance of power in the region so that China would resume an important geopolitical role. During World War II, Roosevelt had always insisted that China should be treated as a great power. Although he became increasingly disappointed with its actual military contribution to the war effort, Roosevelt held fast to the idea that China would act as one of the world's 'four policemen', helping to maintain the postwar peace. The president declared that for more than a century the Chinese people 'have been, in thought and in objective, closer to us Americans than almost any other peoples in the world' (Dallek, 1979, p. 391). In his opinion, a strong and democratic China would speed the advance of economic and political progress throughout the Far East. This favourable image, however, sharply diverged from the reality of an impoverished country bitterly divided by civil war.

The Kuomintang (Guomindang) or Nationalist Party had ruled China since the 1920s. The United States officially recognized the nationalist government in 1928 and entered into alliance with it during World War II. The nationalist leader, Chiang Kai-shek, was particularly admired in the United States, where the China lobby praised his efforts to defend freedom against the fascist menace of Japan. Moreover, Chiang's conversion to Christianity and the fact that his wife had been educated in the United States further enhanced his image as a champion of Western values. On the other hand, the nationalists were known to be notoriously corrupt and inefficient. They were dominated by a military clique whose oppressive rule aroused increasing unrest and provoked a major agrarian revolt, led by the Communist Party under Mao Tse-tung (Mao Zedong). Roosevelt was only too well aware of the dangers of becoming ensnared in the tangle of internal Chinese politics, but he believed that it was essential to maintain Chiang in power if China was to remain in the war. The alternatives of political chaos or a communist regime were unacceptable.

Shortly before the close of the war with Japan in August 1945, Soviet troops entered Manchuria in accordance with the wartime agreement made at the Yalta conference by Roosevelt and Stalin. In China itself, Mao controlled large areas of the northeast and boasted an army of 500,000. The prospect of further communist advances prompted the Truman administration to dispatch 50,000 American marines to help the nationalists re-establish their authority in the important cities of east China and repatriate the defeated Japanese forces. But Chiang's hold on power was extremely precarious. American officials feared the outbreak of a full-scale civil war and sought to avoid this by encouraging the creation of a coalition government. They optimistically believed that the nationalists and communists had cooperated in the past and could do so again.

In December 1945 President Truman sent General Marshall to China with the task of mediating the differences between Chiang and Mao. Although a cease-fire was quickly announced, this proved an empty gesture since the nationalists and communists thoroughly distrusted each other and were not disposed to negotiate a Western-style political compromise. The futility of Marshall's attempted mediation and the limits of American influence were underlined by Chiang's unilateral decision to launch a military offensive against the communists in the northeast. In January 1947 Marshall confessed defeat and complained of the 'almost insurmountable and maddening obstacles to bring some measure of peace to China' (Schlesinger, 1983, IV, p. 125).

American officials believed that Chiang had seriously blundered in renewing the civil war. Acheson privately described the offensive as 'the death wish of the Kuomintang' (Acheson, 1970, p. 203). By 1947, however, China had become a matter of less urgency for American diplomacy. The Soviet menace had markedly receded when Soviet troops were pulled out of Manchuria in the spring of 1946. In fact, Stalin adhered to the peace treaty which he had signed with Chiang in August 1945 and continued to recognize the nationalists as the official government of China. Despite the apparent ideological affinity between Mao and Stalin, Soviet influence was not overtly visible in Chinese affairs. 'There is a good chance', argued George Kennan, 'that if you let the Russians alone in China they will come a cropper on that problem just as everybody else has for hundreds of years' (Kennan, 1968, p. 374).

The Truman administration essentially wished to extricate itself from the China tangle. American marines were withdrawn during 1947 to avoid any possibility of their becoming directly involved in the civil war. A political complication was raised, however, by Chiang's skill in mobilizing the support of the 'China lobby' in Washington. Posing as the 'co-defender of democracy', Chiang astutely appealed for American aid 'against the onrush and infiltration of Communism throughout the world' (Schlesinger, 1983, IV, p. 155). While the Truman administration dared not 'abandon' Chiang, it would only grant him limited economic and military aid. To defeat the Chinese communists, Marshall explained, 'it would be necessary for the United States virtually to take over the Chinese Government and administer its economic, military and governmental affairs' (Schlesinger, 1983, IV, p. 154). The idea of such a massive American commitment had always been rejected. Moreover, the stark reality of China's economic and political chaos removed the pretence that the country was a model of democracy or that it warranted great-power status. Since China could not conceivably be considered a military threat to the United States, the Far East was downgraded in strategic importance. American officials directed their attention to what they considered to be the much more pressing threat of communism in Europe.

In 1949, however, the military stalemate in China was dramatically broken. The communists advanced from their base in Manchuria and overran the mainland. In October 1949 Mao formally proclaimed the establishment of the People's Republic of China (PRC or Red China). By the end of the year Chiang had retreated to the island of Formosa (Taiwan). The Truman administration was confounded by the turn of events but not altogether surprised. American officials were instructed to remain in China and it seemed that diplomatic relations might soon be established with the new regime. In August 1949 Secretary of State Acheson had sought to explain American policy by releasing to Congress a selection of important documents known as the *China White Paper*. In his opinion:

> The unfortunate but inescapable fact is that the ominous result of the civil war in China was beyond the control of the government of the United States. Nothing that this country did or could have done within the reasonable limits of its capabilities could have changed that result; nothing that was left undone by this country has

contributed to it. It was the product of internal Chinese forces, forces which this country tried to influence but could not. (Acheson, 1970, p. 303)

Acheson later recalled that the *China White Paper* was greeted 'by a storm of abuse from very diverse groups in the Congress and the press' (Acheson, 1970, p. 303). Critics were disturbed and infuriated by the implication that a country as powerful as the United States had been incapable of preventing Chiang's downfall. They also pointed out that Acheson's complacent acceptance of the primacy of 'internal Chinese forces' was a direct acknowledgment of communist control over the country. One group of American senators issued a public statement condemning the document as a '1,054 page whitewash of a wishful, do-nothing policy which has succeeded in placing Asia in danger of Soviet conquest with its ultimate threat to the peace of the world and of our own national security' (Graebner, 1984, p. 169).

The timing of the document was unfortunate for the Truman administration in coming so soon after the war scare over the Berlin blockade. It also coincided with the formation of NATO and the news of the Soviet explosion of an atomic bomb. Consequently, many Americans readily attached a global significance to events in China. Rather than an indigenous rising against a notoriously oppressive and corrupt regime, the communist victory was interpreted as part of the world conspiracy directed from Moscow. The Chinese communist leaders were merely tools who obediently served the interests of Soviet imperialism. This suspicion was seemingly confirmed by Mao's visit to Moscow in December 1949 followed by the signing of the Sino-Soviet treaty of Alliance in February 1950.

Republican critics joined with the 'China lobby' to berate the Democratic administration for doing too little for Chiang and therefore 'losing' China. But it was not only incompetence that was singled out for blame. The Truman administration was accused of assuming a cowardly direction because it contained traitors who manipulated policy in the interests of the Soviet Union. Fear of infiltration by 'reds' had already prompted investigations by the federal government and Congress of 'loyalty' and 'un-American activities'. The mood turned to national paranoia when the theme was vigorously taken up by Senator Joe McCarthy of Wisconsin.

In a speech at Wheeling, West Virginia, in February 1950, McCarthy claimed that he possessed the names of known communists who were currently employed in the State Department. McCarthy was unable to substantiate his charges, but his speeches had an amazing impact on American public opinion. The subsequent upsurge of 'McCarthyism' transformed the 'loss' of China into a powerful and emotive political issue. The area of mainland China under communist control was pejoratively called 'Red China'. Moreover, its government was considered to be an inveterate enemy of the United States. Consequently, the question of recognizing the new regime was abruptly dumped as American officials sought to prove that they had never been nor would they ever be 'soft' on communism. In the process, China became an active participant and integral element in the Cold War struggle between the superpowers.

The Korean War

Surrounded by powerful neighbours, the people of the Korean peninsula were long accustomed to external interference in their domestic affairs. At the turn of the twentieth century, control of the region was fiercely contested between China, Russia and Japan. The latter was ultimately victorious and incorporated Korea within the Japanese empire from 1910 until 1945. The United States tacitly acquiesced in Japan's ascendancy and showed little interest in Korea until World War II. Because it was one of the victims of Japanese aggression, Roosevelt believed that Korea should become independent at the end of the war. But no discussion was undertaken as to how this might be implemented. After Japan's surrender in 1945, Soviet troops crossed into northern Korea from neighbouring Siberia. The United States was militarily unprepared, but wished to prevent the Soviet Union from absorbing the whole of Korea by default. American troops were therefore airlifted to the south of the country and a dividing line between the two armies was arbitrarily drawn at the 38th parallel.

Both the United States and the Soviet Union affirmed their aim of establishing a united and independent Korea. A mutual withdrawal of the occupying forces was agreed, although this was not fully implemented until 1949. In the meantime the political divisions within Korea were so intractable that it proved impossible to unify the country either by organizing national elections or by establishing a trustee system supervised by the United Nations. Consequently, the temporary dividing line of the 38th parallel became fixed and separated the country into two antagonistic rival states. In the north, the communists were dominant and formed the Democratic People's Republic of Korea (North Korea). Its leader was the Marxist revolutionary, Kim Il Sung, who had spent World War II in the Soviet Union. In marked contrast, the southern leader, Syngman Rhee, had lived in America for more than 30 years. Although Rhee was a staunch nationalist, he closely aligned the Republic of Korea (ROK or South Korea) with the United States. The tensions of the Cold War were replicated in Korea as Kim and Rhee vilified each other for causing the division of the country. Both leaders declared that they would bring about reunification by whatever means were necessary, including the use of force. A state of undeclared civil war ensued in which several thousand Koreans were killed.

In January 1950 the Korean question became entwined with that of China. Responding to public anxiety over American intentions towards Taiwan, President Truman informed the press that the United States had no intention of interfering militarily to protect Chiang. A week later in a celebrated speech delivered at the Washington Press Club, Secretary of State Acheson sought to clarify the president's remarks by stating that American strategy in the Far East was unchanged. He stressed that America's military power in the region depended upon maintaining a string of naval and air bases running across the Pacific from the Aleutians to Japan, the Ryukyus and the Philippines. These islands formed the nation's front line of defence. By implication, other countries such as Taiwan and South Korea lay outside what was described as America's 'defensive perimeter' (Schlesinger, 1983, IV, p. 362).

Although Roosevelt and Truman had supplied Chiang with financial aid and military equipment, they had never been willing to send American troops to fight to ensure his political survival. According to Acheson's speech, it looked as if the United States would not even contest an invasion of Taiwan by the Chinese communists. So long as America was searching its soul over the 'loss' of China, the military initiative in the Far East appeared to rest with the communists. Mao declared that Americans had suffered a 'loss of face' and that the United States was no more than 'a paper tiger' (Ulam, 1973, p. 165). Hostilities erupted, however, not, as expected in Taiwan, but further to the north in Korea where the Soviet Union had been helping Kim Il Sung to prepare the North Korean army and air force for a major offensive. With the apparent approval of Stalin, Kim ordered his forces to invade South Korea on 25 June 1950. His proclaimed intention was to bring an end to the state of undeclared civil war, 'liberate' the South and thereby reunify the two Koreas.

The exclusion of Korea from Acheson's definition of America's 'defensive perimeter' gave Stalin and Kim good reason to believe that the United States would remain passive as North Korean forces absorbed the whole peninsula. The Truman administration, how-ever, chose to reverse its policy of military disengagement from the Asian mainland. Kim's initiative was not attributed to internal Korean politics. Under the influence of McCarthyism and the warnings of communist global conspiracy contained in NSC-68, American officials were convinced that the Soviets had deliberately planned the invasion to test the resolve of the West. In fact, other aggressive communist moves were anticipated in Southeast Asia and especially in Europe, where Berlin and Yugoslavia were considered to be the most likely targets. On receiving news of the crisis by telephone, Truman immediately flew from Missouri to Washington. He later recalled:

> I had time to think aboard the plane, In my generation, this was not the first occasion when the strong had attacked the weak. I recalled some earlier instances: Manchuria, Ethiopia, Austria. I remembered how each time that the democracies failed to act it had encouraged the aggressors to keep going ahead. Communism was acting in Korea just as Hitler, Mussolini, and the Japanese had acted ten, fifteen, and twenty years earlier ... If this was allowed to go unchallenged it would mean a third world war, just as similar incidents had brought on a second world war. (Truman, 1956, p. 351)

Truman placed events in an international and historical perspec-tive. He was determined that there should be no repetition of the policy of appeasement which was now seen as having been so disastrous during the 1930s. 'This is the Greece of the Far East', the president told his staff (May, 1973, p. 71). The defence of South Korea was accordingly considered as vital to America's national security. But there was no NATO or military alliance that South Korea could invoke and ask assistance from. Since the United States was not under attack, the American Congress could hardly declare a state of war. Truman therefore requested an immediate meeting of the Security Council of the United Nations. Assisted by the fortuitous absence of the Soviet representative, whose government was currently boycotting the Security Council, the American delegation secured the unanimous adoption of a resolution calling upon North Korea to withdraw its forces from South Korea. A second resolution was passed two days later asking members of the United Nations to provide troops to drive back the invaders. On 27 June 1950 Truman announced that the United States would comply with the resolution and deploy its military forces on behalf of the United Nations. In reality, however, it was an 'American' war. Although 16 nations eventually sent troops, the American contribution was so much the largest – amounting to half the number of combat troops and 80–90 per cent of air and naval support – that the various contingents were unified under American control and direction. General MacArthur was transferred from Japan to assume command.

During the first weeks of fighting, the North Koreans virtually overran the whole peninsula, but were unable to achieve complete military victory. In September MacArthur brilliantly outflanked the enemy by making an amphibious landing several hundred miles to the north at Inchon. The North Korean forces were cut in half and were soon in headlong retreat. The United Nations (UN) forces proceeded to cross the 38th parallel and steadily advanced to the Yalu River, which marked the North Korean border with China. The original mission to resist aggression was thereby deliberately changed to include the conquest of North Korea. MacArthur confidently predicted that neither the Soviets nor China would join the war, but he was proved grievously wrong with respect to China when that country launched a major offensive involving 200,000 troops in November. Only a few weeks earlier a Chinese newspaper had warned: 'We cannot stand idly by when the American imperialist, a notorious enemy, is now expanding its war of aggression against our neighbor and is attempting to extend the aggressive flames to the borders of the country' (Kaufman, 1986, p. 93). The Chinese intervention destroyed American hopes of a successful end of the war by Christmas 1950. It was now the turn of the UN forces to retreat. A prolonged war of attrition was conducted in which the lines of battle moved back and forth until both sides consolidated their respective positions close to the same 38th parallel that had marked the prewar border.

In the meantime, MacArthur clashed with Truman over military tactics and was removed from his command for exceeding his instructions. The president refused to expand the war beyond Korea and ruled out retaliatory air strikes against China. Truman's caution had already been demonstrated earlier, in December 1950, when he responded to the appeals of the British prime minister, Clement Attlee, to withdraw the veiled threat to use atomic weapons. By deliberately 'limiting' the war, however, Truman abandoned the goal of seeking total victory over North Korea and indicated that he was willing to accept a territorial settlement that broadly reflected the prewar status quo. The strategy of 'limited war' resulted, however, in a military stalemate that dragged on for several months and proved not only costly in casualties but also an increasing political liability for the Truman administration. During the presidential election campaign in 1952, the Republican candidate, Dwight Eisenhower, correctly perceived the growing disenchantment of American public opinion. His pledge 'to go to Korea' implied that he had a plan to end the war and contributed significantly to his election victory. Shortly after assuming office, Eisenhower made it known that he was prepared to use atomic weapons against China. This threat combined with the change in Soviet leadership caused by the death of Stalin in March and the evident war-weariness on all sides to bring about a cease-fire signed at Panmunjom in July 1953. The agreement essentially recognized the existing battle-line and prewar borders. Although provision was made for future conferences to discuss reunification, the politics of the Cold War ensured that the peninsula would remain divided at the 38th parallel. North Korea stayed firmly within the communist orbit, while South Korea became closely tied to the United States.

The decision to intervene militarily in 1950 reflected Truman's belief that communism must be contained globally. But such an ambitious strategy was prohibitively expensive and risky. To widen the war beyond Korea would not only be enormously costly, but might also bring about the third world war that Truman was trying to avoid in the first place. The dilemma was highlighted by General Omar Bradley's celebrated statement that the conflict in Korea must not become 'the wrong war, at the wrong place, at the wrong time and with the wrong enemy' (Bartlett, 1994, p. 300). Convinced that the invasion was part of a Soviet conspiracy, American officials feared a similar attack in Europe. Indeed, sending troops to fight in Korea was designed to impress not only America's communist foes but also its European friends. So much diplomatic effort was expended to persuade the European allies to build up their conventional forces and to accept German rearmament that at times the military struggle in Korea became a virtual sideshow.

Nevertheless, the Korean War demonstrated that American officials considered the containment of communism to be a global struggle and not just applicable to Europe. Despite the lack of tangible evidence, the Chinese entry into the war was interpreted as confirmation that 'Red' China was under the control of the Soviet Union. 'The Mao Tse-tung regime is a creature of the Moscow Politburo', declared John Foster Dulles (Graebner, 1984, p. 180). Although thirteen countries, including Britain, had established diplomatic relations with the new Chinese government before June 1950, the United States refused to grant recognition. A policy of isolating Red China was adopted. Commercial and cultural relations were prohibited. At the United Nations, the American delegation resolutely opposed Red China's membership and secured the passage of a resolution condemning that government's aggression in Korea. The United States continued to recognize the nationalists in Taiwan as the legitimate government of China. Consequently, Taiwan (Republic of China) retained its seat on the Security Council, although it represented only 13 million out of a total Chinese population in excess of 500 million.

In January 1950 the Truman administration had implied that Taiwan lay outside America's defensive perimeter. Less than six months later the president affirmed that 'the occupation of Formosa by Communist forces would be a direct threat to the security of the Pacific area' (Schlesinger, 1983, IV, p. 366). The powerful American Seventh Fleet was sent to patrol the Taiwan Strait to forestall a possible invasion from the mainland. Considerable military and financial assistance was given to Chiang so that he was able to maintain himself in power and also to transform Taiwan into a formidable military stronghold. In December 1954 communist threats to seize the small islands of Quemoy and Matsu situated in the Taiwan Strait so alarmed the Eisenhower administration that it speedily entered into a defence treaty by which the United States gave a formal pledge to protect Taiwan.

The war in Korea also radically altered American relations with the other nations of the Far East. In Japan, the United States expedited the conclusion of a peace treaty in 1951 to end the occupation and restore Japanese independence. The new government of Japan immediately entered into a bilateral security agreement with the United States by which American forces were to remain in Japan for an indefinite period to provide for the nation's defence. Prior to the Korean War, George Kennan had advocated American military withdrawal from Japan, but he later concluded that 'the American military presence in Japan was wholly essential to any future security of the area' (Kennan, 1968, p. 396). For half a century the United States had sought to build up China to curb Japanese expansionism. After 1950 American policy stressed the importance of allying with Japan in order to contain the spread of Chinese communism.

Meanwhile the United States sought to establish a powerful anti-communist coalition. Defence treaties were signed with Australia, New Zealand and the Philippines in 1951. The Eisenhower administration made the structure more formal in September 1954 by creating the Manila Pact or South East Asia Treaty Organization (SEATO). Intended as a Far Eastern counterpart to NATO, the new regional defence organization comprised the United States, Britain, France, Australia, New Zealand, Pakistan, Thailand and the Philippines. In contrast to NATO, however, the treaty did not provide for an automatic commitment by its signatories to use force to resist aggression. Such a stipulation would have placed an enormous burden upon the United States since that country possessed the most substantial military forces. The members of SEATO simply agreed to confer in the event 'of any fact or situation which might endanger the peace of the area' (Schlesinger, 1983, IV, p. 474). The limits of the alliance were further underlined by the conspicuous refusal to join of leading regional powers such as India and Indonesia.

Almost 34,000 Americans had died in the Korean War, while the number of Koreans and Chinese killed, injured and missing numbered more than three million. Since the country still remained divided at the 38th parallel, the fighting appeared to have achieved little except wreaking further destruction upon an already unfortunate people. Although the United States claimed to be fighting a monolithic communist conspiracy directed from Moscow, the Soviet Union carefully avoided direct military involvement. Whether Red China acted independently or was manipulated by the Soviets into joining the war, the consequences for subsequent Sino-American relations were disastrous. During the next two decades the United States and Red China were implacable enemies. The alliance system devised by the United States to isolate Red China appeared to signify a dramatic reversal of America's traditional policy of avoiding military commitments in the Far East. America had stood up to the perceived communist challenge in Korea and it might be argued that Truman's resolute action had prevented a local conflict from expanding into a third world war. But American power had failed to win a decisive military victory on the battlefield. Furthermore, the experience of fighting a 'limited war' was financially and politically debilitating. A similar saga was repeated in Vietnam, where the results proved to be just as frustrating and ultimately more disastrous for the United States.

The Vietnamese Domino

By the close of the nineteenth century the region of Southeast Asia had become a French sphere of influence. The centre of France's Asian empire was Indochina, comprising the kingdoms of Cambodia and Laos, and the three Vietnamese provinces of Tonkin, Annam and Cochin China. The colony was considered highly attractive because it was naturally rich in rice and rubber. It also provided an opportunity to promote France's 'civilizing mission' of instilling its language, traditions and culture overseas. French domination endured until 1940, when it was dramatically overthrown by Japan's military onslaught, which temporarily swept away white colonial rule throughout most of East Asia.

Already demoralized by their country's defeat at the hands of Germany in Europe, the French officials who administered the government of Indochina obediently surrendered to the Japanese invaders. However, by choosing collaboration rather than resistance, French authority and prestige were fatally compromised in Indochina. Active local opposition to the Japanese was mainly confined to the area close to the Chinese border in Tonkin, where guerrilla warfare was organized by a communist movement known as the Vietnam Independence League or Vietminh. Guided by the charismatic Ho Chi Minh and the military genius of Vo Nguyen Giap, the Vietminh emerged as a formidable political and military force in Tonkin. Their aim was not only to resist the Japanese but also to bring an end to French colonial rule in the Vietnamese provinces.

After the liberation of France from German occupation in 1944, rumours circulated that French troops would be shortly sent from Europe to reconquer Indochina. Japan reacted in March 1945 by forcibly dismissing the local French administration. Annam, Tonkin and Cochin China were declared united in the new state of Vietnam, which was given nominal independence under the rule of Bao Dai, the emperor of Annam. But Japan's plans to mobilize anti-French feeling were shattered by its own military surrender to the United States in August. Ho moved rapidly to fill the resulting vacuum of political power in the Vietnamese provinces. Claiming to represent nationalist aspirations for independence from foreign rule, Vietminh forces entered Hanoi, the principal city in the north, and established a government in the name of the newly created Democratic Republic of Vietnam (DRV).

The bold act of declaring an independent republic gained support only within northern Vietnam and attracted virtually no international notice. Realizing that the United States was the most influential foreign power in the region, Ho shrewdly appealed for its support. He told an American secret agent that he would welcome 'a million American soldiers . . . but no French'. In similar vein, General Giap described the United States as a 'good friend' because 'it is a democracy without territorial ambitions' (Karnow, 1984, p. 147). This image of the United States as a friendly and disinterested power derived from President Roosevelt's well-known opposition to the restoration of French sovereignty in Indochina. On one memorable occasion, he had denounced France for having 'done nothing for the Indochinese people under their care' (Thorne, 1978, p. 463).

Roosevelt's anti-colonial attitude was sincere, but it was moderated by his desire for French assistance to end the war against Japan. Shortly before his death, the president even sanctioned the use of American planes to airlift small detachments of French troops within Indochina. Moreover, the vital importance of American support to France was stressed by the leader of the Free French Forces in France, Charles de Gaulle, who ominously warned the American ambassador at Paris in March 1945:

> If the public here comes to realize that you are against us in Indochina there will be terrific disappointment and nobody knows to what that will lead. We do not want to become Communist; we do not want to fall into the Russian orbit, but I hope that you will not push us into it. (Thorne, 1978, p. 622)

Lacking Roosevelt's personal interest in Asian affairs, Truman was even less inclined to make Indochina a divisive issue between the United States and France. Indeed, the new president was only too pleased to receive assurances from de Gaulle that France intended to grant independence to its colonies, even though this 'would inevitably be varied and gradual' (Herring, 1979, p. 111). Wishing to endorse France's claims to great-power status, the Truman administration ignored Ho's appeals for assistance and chose instead to acquiesce in the restoration of French rule in Indochina. The opportunity to investigate the possibilities for cooperation between the Vietminh and the United States government was therefore missed.

At first the French authorities were willing to consider granting a measure of local self-government to the Vietminh. Ho even visited Paris for discussions on this subject during the summer of 1946. However, friction between the Vietminh and French troops in the northern port city of Haiphong erupted into violence in November 1946 and during the following month sparked off the 'First Indochina War', which lasted until 1954. It was a struggle of attrition in which neither side showed any disposition to compromise. The Vietminh dedicated themselves to achieving the independence of a unified Vietnam. The French government declared its determination to reimpose its colonial authority. Outwardly, France appeared to be winning the war. The French administration in Indochina remained intact and control was retained over the populated urban areas. But the influence of the Vietminh grew steadily throughout Tonkin, especially among the peasants in the countryside. Moreover, the successful guerrilla tactics employed by the Vietminh caused a constant drain of lives and money that made the war increasingly unpopular in France. In 1954 the French commander, General Henri Navarre, sought a decisive test of military strength at Dien Bien Phu, a remote garrison in the northwest. But he was outmanoeuvred and outnumbered by Giap. The surrender of Dien Bien Phu in May 1954 brought down the French government and marked the end of France's forlorn attempt to hold on to its empire in Indochina.

Although consenting to the restoration of French rule in 1945, the Truman administration had displayed little interest in the region. American officials remained suspicious of the Vietminh, whom they considered to be not nationalists but Soviet puppets. On the other hand, there was scant sympathy for French colonialism, so that requests for American military assistance against the Vietminh were refused. This negative attitude was dramatically altered by the 'loss' of China in 1949 and the outbreak of the Korean War during the following year. In American eyes, Indochina was no longer the scene of a purely local conflict, but an integral part of the global battle to contain Soviet expansion. The Cold War perspective was further reinforced by the decision of Red China and the Soviet Union to grant diplomatic recognition to the Vietminh in 1950. Consequently, from 1950 onwards the United States began a programme of financial assistance to France, which was steadily increased until it amounted to almost 80 per cent of French expenditure on the war.

Shocked by the turn of events in China, American officials were anxious over the possible 'loss' to communism of any further countries in Asia. This fear gained the name of the 'domino theory' after President Eisenhower's remarks at a press conference in April 1954. He stated: 'You have a row of dominoes set up, you knock over the first one, and what will happen to the last one is the certainty that it will go over very quickly. So you could have a beginning of a disintegration that would have the most profound influence' (Ambrose, 1984, p. 180). Speaking as Dien Bien Phu was under siege, Eisenhower had Indochina very much in mind. Implicit in his remarks was that the fall of Indochina would be followed by similar communist successes in neighbouring Burma, Thailand, Malaya and Indonesia. After Southeast Asia, communist pressure would extend to Japan, Taiwan and the Philippines. The next dominoes would be Australia, New Zealand and ultimately the United States itself.

Despite this alarming scenario, caution still prevailed in Washington. Both Truman and Eisenhower drew a sharp distinction between financial aid and direct American military involvement in Indochina. Confronted with desperate pleas from Paris for an American air strike to save the beleaguered French garrison at Dien Bien Phu, Eisenhower sought not only the opinion of his military experts and leading congressmen, but also the cooperation of the British government. Several American officials, including Dulles, favoured an air strike. After careful consideration, Eisenhower ruled against military intervention. 'We cannot engage in active war', he told Dulles (Ambrose, 1984, p. 179).

The decision provoked French bitterness, but was not quite as momentous as it appeared because the French government had already indicated its desire to negotiate a withdrawal from Indochina. In February 1954 it had agreed to join a conference of foreign ministers scheduled to meet at Geneva in July to discuss peace in Indochina. Dulles was initially reluctant to attend, primarily because he regarded with distaste the presence of a delegation from Red China. Ironically, the Chinese foreign minister, Chou En-lai (Zhou Enlai), exercised a moderating influence throughout the proceedings. After the sacrifices of the Korean War, China yearned for peace and was also wary of creating an overpowerful Vietnam on its border. Moreover, the Soviet delegates too displayed a conciliatory attitude at the conference. The Soviet Union was actually more concerned about developments in Europe than in Indochina and wished to avoid antagonizing French opinion in the debate currently raging in France over the EDC. Consequently, the demands of the Vietminh representative for an independent and unified Vietnam were regarded as too extreme and he was prevailed upon to accept a number of 'accords' with the French government. These stipulated an end to hostilities and the division of Vietnam at the 17th parallel into what would become the separate states of 'North' and 'South' Vietnam. The division, however, was regarded as temporary pending national elections to be held within two years. It was envisaged that French troops would be withdrawn by July 1956.

While not displeased by the end of French colonial rule in Indochina, the Eisenhower administration was unhappy at the 'loss' of northern Vietnam to communism. The American delegation at Geneva implied its assent to the accords, although it refused to grant them a formal endorsement. A statement was issued that the United States 'would view any renewal of the aggression in violation of the

aforesaid agreements with grave concern and as seriously threatening international peace and security' (*New York Times*, 1971, p. 52).
In fact, the assertion that the United States possessed a protective
interest in the future of Vietnam reflected the unilateral decision of
the Eisenhower administration to replace the French in Indochina.
The detached policy of the past was abandoned as Eisenhower and
Dulles imposed the politics of the Cold War upon Vietnam. Their
declared aim was to defeat the domino theory by creating a strong
and stable non-Communist nation in the South which would serve
as a beacon of freedom in the region.

By treating South Vietnam as a separate and sovereign state, the
United States deliberately undermined the intention of the Geneva
settlement to unite the two Vietnams. 'While we should certainly
take no positive step to speed up [the] present process of decay of
[the] Geneva accords,' remarked Dulles in December 1955, 'neither
should we make the slightest effort to infuse life into them' (*New
York Times*, 1971, p. 23). The stipulation that Vietnam could not
enter into a foreign alliance was circumvented by the inclusion of
a separate protocol in the SEATO treaty of September 1954
extending its protection to Vietnam. An American military mission
took over from the French in 1956 and proceeded to train and equip
what was intended to be a powerful South Vietnamese army (Army
of the Republic of Vietnam or ARVN). In this way, the United
States consciously entered what would eventually become known as
the 'quagmire' of Vietnam.

American policy also sought to promote political stability by
approving Ngo Dinh Diem's establishment of an independent Republic of Vietnam (RVN or South Vietnam) in October 1955. Fearful that
national elections would result in a communist victory, America made
no objection to Diem's ingenious declaration that South Vietnam had
not signed the Geneva accords and was not therefore obliged to hold
elections. Instead, Diem preferred to stage his own 'national referen-
dum', in which he won 98 per cent of the vote, including 605,000 votes
from the 405,000 voters registered in the capital city, Saigon! On his
state visit to Washington in May 1957 Diem was met at the airport by
Eisenhower and warmly welcomed as a redoubtable ally in the struggle
against international communism.

The praise bestowed upon Diem by Eisenhower for inspiring
national unity and making 'notable progress towards the great
goal of constitutional government' illustrated how misinformed

Americans were about the nature of the political system in South Vietnam (Schlesinger, 1983, IV, p. 478). Diem's patriotism and anti-communism were not in doubt, but he was also personally a tyrant whose nepotism and devout Catholicism exacerbated Vietnamese political, religious and cultural divisions. In October 1957 a renewal of guerrilla activity was reported in the countryside. In essence, this marked the beginning of the 'Second Indochina War', which continued until 1975. By 1959 North Vietnamese military supplies and advisers were infiltrating the South via a series of paths and tracks through the jungle that became known as 'the Ho Chi Minh Trail'. Successfully exploiting Diem's unpopularity, the guerrillas steadily expanded their influence in the rural villages. In 1960 they called themselves the National Liberation Front (NLF) and declared that their aim was to overthrow Diem and reunify Vietnam. In the South, the NLF was given the name 'Vietcong' (VC).

Although the Eisenhower administration was alarmed by the growing level of violence reported in South Vietnam, it was more directly concerned over events in Europe, especially the Berlin crisis. Indeed, as Eisenhower left office in January 1961, he made only a passing reference about Vietnam to his successor. Nevertheless, President John F. Kennedy soon became closely involved in Vietnamese affairs. It was clear from his inaugural address that he intended to be an activist president in foreign affairs. Moreover, Vietnam suddenly acquired special significance early in his administration as a result of a series of international crises occurring in Cuba, Laos and Berlin. Coming away from the Vienna summit meeting with Khrushchev in July 1961, Kennedy believed that America's credibility as leader of the free world was in question. 'Now we have a problem in making our power credible, and Vietnam is the place', he told an American reporter (Karnow, 1984, p. 248).

Assisted by an administration that contained some of the 'best and brightest' minds of their generation, Kennedy approached the task more as a challenge than a burden. Indeed, Vietnam presented an opportunity to implement the fashionable strategy of 'flexible response', in which communist guerrillas would be destroyed by counter-insurgency operations. Teams of American 'advisers', including 'Special Forces' troops known as 'Green Berets', were sent to teach the new tactics to the South Vietnamese army. Emphasis was placed not on direct combat against the enemy, but on going into the countryside to win the 'hearts and minds' of the peasants. Despite official optimism, the initial results of the 'strategic hamlet program' were disappointing. More and more American military assistance was required, even extending to the provision of tactical air support for the South Vietnamese army. The number of American advisers serving in South Vietnam markedly increased, from 685 in 1961 to almost 16,000 in 1963.

The dilemma facing American policy was summed up in two televised interviews given by President Kennedy in September 1963. In words reminiscent of Acheson's *China White Paper*, Kennedy emphasized the critical role of the people of Vietnam:

> In the final analysis, it is their war. They are the ones who have to win it or lose it. We can help them, we can give them equipment, we can send our men out there as advisers, but they have to win it – the people of Vietnam – against the Communists. (Schlesinger, 1983, IV, p. 483).

A week later, when asked whether he believed in the domino theory, the president replied:

> I believe it. I think that the struggle is close enough. China is so large, looms so high just beyond the frontiers, that if South Vietnam went, it would not only give them an improved geographic position for a guerrilla assault on Malaya but would also give the impression that the wave of the future in Southeast Asia was China and the Communists. So I believe it. (Schlesinger, 1983, IV, p. 484)

Whatever his own personal misgivings, the 'loss' of China still exercised a powerful influence upon Kennedy and made him feel obliged to subscribe to the rhetoric of the Cold War. He judged that withdrawal from South Vietnam would destroy America's credibility overseas and rekindle McCarthyism at home. His decision to protect the South from communism by significantly increasing American military involvement only served, however, to intensify the fighting and ensured that the United States sank further into the quagmire of Vietnam.

Kennedy secretly feared that American intervention might expand to such an extent that an internal Asian conflict would be transformed into an 'American' war. This stage was reached not during his own presidency but during that of his successor, Lyndon Johnson. On assuming office after Kennedy's assassination in

November 1963, Johnson reacted to gloomy military reports from South Vietnam with the declaration that he had no intention of being 'the first American President to lose a war' (Graebner, 1984, p. 234). Johnson, however, did not seek an official congressional declaration of war in order to launch a full-scale invasion and conquest of North Vietnam. Instead, an undeclared 'war' was conducted in which the United States sought to punish North Vietnam for its aggression against the South. This would be achieved by gradually escalating the fighting on the ground and especially in the air until the enemy was forced to admit defeat. A negotiated settlement was not offered. Like Roosevelt against Germany in World War II, Johnson demanded the unconditional surrender of North Vietnam and the Vietcong. In 1964 he ordered the first of many massive bombing raids on North Vietnam. Operation 'Rolling Thunder' lasted for more than three years and resulted in 600,000 tons of bombs being dropped on the North. In 1965 the first battalions of American ground forces were dispatched to South Vietnam. Adopting the tactics of 'search and destroy', American troops quickly assumed a direct combat role against the Vietcong. By 1968 more than 500,000 American servicemen were stationed in South Vietnam. In the process, the war was effectively 'Americanized'.

Johnson hoped to win the war quickly at minimum financial cost. In 1965 his advisers estimated that America's military effort would require an annual expenditure of $2 billion. Within two years the United States was spending this same amount per month! Moreover, despite optimistic official reports, the expected military victory was not forthcoming. What was a 'limited' war for the United States was a 'total' war for North Vietnam. 'The Vietnamese people will never give way to force', defiantly asserted Ho Chi Minh (Schlesinger, 1983, IV, p. 519). Moreover, the American faith in the efficacy of strategic bombing proved misplaced. The predominantly agrarian economy of North Vietnam presented few significant targets for American air strikes. American bombing was also selective and, for example, rarely attacked the principal North Vietnamese cities of Hanoi and Haiphong. Instead of lowering the enemy's morale, the policy of escalation merely stimulated North Vietnamese determination to continue the war and to increase infiltration into the South. Saturation bombing by B-52s looked impressive, but was surprisingly ineffective in closing the supply routes along the Ho Chi Minh Trail. Even American officials admitted that the number of North Vietnamese troops entering the South actually tripled from 1965 to 1967.

As Johnson escalated the war, the American presence in South Vietnam became so overwhelming that the authority of the government in Saigon was critically undermined. Moreover, the assassination of Diem in 1963 had resulted in a succession of political crises and military coups. Although Americans had initially supported Johnson's policy of escalation, they soon began to question why their country was fighting to preserve a repressive government which did not even appear to have the support of its own people. Furthermore, American consciousness of the war was heightened not only by the mounting cost in casualties and money but also by television newsreels which conveyed daily pictures of brutality and horror. Incidents such as the dropping of napalm by American planes and the slaughter of women and children at the hamlet of My Lai by American marines provoked a sense of moral confusion and outrage. By the presidential election year of 1968 criticism of America's involvement in the war resounded through-out Congress and the media. Large anti-war demonstrations were organized in American cities and on college campuses. Particular anger was directed at the indiscriminate nature of American bombing in Vietnam. A frequent chant used by protestors outside the White House was: 'Hey, hey, LBJ, how many kids have you killed today?'

Since the enunciation of the Truman Doctrine in 1947, American foreign policy had enjoyed the support of American public opinion. This Cold War 'consensus' collapsed, however, amid the traumatic experience that Americans simply and ruefully referred to as 'Vietnam'. A 'credibility gap' emerged over the truthfulness of statements made by government officials. If South Vietnam was so crucial to the defence of the United States, critics asked, why had the president not asked Congress to declare a state of war against North Vietnam? Moreover, the domino theory, which had been so persuasive during the 1950s, was no longer regarded as axiomatic. Americans found it difficult to believe that the real enemies were the Soviet Union and China. Both these powers were known to be engaged in their own bitter ideological dispute with each other. Although they gave considerable assistance to North Vietnam, this stopped short of direct military participation. Indeed, it was to the advantage of the communist powers to refrain from provocative actions and merely watch the United States suffer increasing international criticism and sink further into the Vietnamese quagmire.

With the exception of the case of Korea in 1950, American presidents had consistently sought to avoid committing American troops to a war on the Asian mainland. Johnson's reversal of this tradition proved a disastrous miscalculation. The president viewed the struggle in Vietnam as a 'limited' war in which America's greatly superior power would soon prevail. The enemy, however, was much more formidable than had been anticipated. Despite suffering enormous losses and damage, North Vietnam and the Vietcong remained resolutely committed to the struggle for national liberation and the unification of Vietnam. 'We will not grow tired', Johnson had declared in April 1965 (Schlesinger, 1983, IV, p. 496). But it was the United States that found the cost of escalation unacceptable. The turning point came in January 1968 when the Vietcong launched the Tet Offensive to coincide with the lunar new year's holiday. The surprise attack was beaten back with heavy Vietcong losses, but not before television pictures had shown their soldiers actually attacking the American embassy in Saigon. Consequently, 'Tet' dealt an enormous psychological blow to American confidence about winning the war.

The mood of growing self-doubt extended to the highest levels of the Johnson administration. More than twenty years earlier Clark Clifford had advised President Truman to be prepared to go to war against the Soviet Union. As secretary of defence in March 1968 he informed President Johnson that he did not believe that a 'conventional military victory' could be achieved in Vietnam. Clifford noted: 'We seem to have gotten caught in a sinkhole. We put in more, they match it . . . and no end [is] in sight' (Clifford, 1991, p. 495). A forlorn President Johnson felt compelled to reverse the policy of escalation and, for the first time, publicly announced America's willingness to seek 'peace through negotiation' (Schlesinger, 1983, IV, p. 536). North Vietnam responded positively and peace talks were started in Paris in May 1968. However, little progress was made because both sides showed no disposition to compromise. By declaring that he would not be a candidate in the 1968 presidential election, Johnson had turned himself into a 'lame duck'. Consequently, the North Vietnamese representatives had little incentive to enter into substantive negotiations with an administration whose days in office were limited.

It was therefore left to Johnson's successor, Richard Nixon, to bring an end to American military involvement in Vietnam. The new president favoured the strategy of 'Vietnamization', in which the American military presence was to be steadily decreased while the burden of fighting the Vietcong was transferred to the South Vietnamese army. At the same time peace discussions were also conducted at Paris to secure a negotiated settlement. But fierce fighting still continued in South Vietnam. Concerned that the North Vietnamese leadership interpreted the policy of Vietnamization as American weakness, Nixon resorted to demonstrations of force in the form of massive air strikes on North Vietnam and enemy 'sanctuaries' located in the neighbouring 'neutral' countries of Laos and Cambodia. In April 1970 American troops invaded Cambodia to destroy the sanctuaries. 'The purpose', explained Nixon, 'was not to expand the war into Cambodia, but to end the war in Vietnam by making peace possible' (Nixon, 1978, p. 452). The decision, however, provoked a wave of public protests throughout the United States, most notably on 4 May at Kent State University, Ohio, where four students were shot and killed by National Guardsmen. Nixon responded by promising a speedy withdrawal of American troops from Cambodia and an acceleration of Vietnamization. Nevertheless, the fighting in the South dragged on and was punctuated with American air strikes against the North, including 'Linebacker I' in May 1972 and 'Linebacker II' in December 1972, involving direct raids on Hanoi and the mining of Haiphong harbour. The 'Christmas Bombing' of Linebacker II was the biggest single bombing operation of the war and provoked a furore of criticism against Nixon, but he argued that it was the only way to convince the North Vietnamese to negotiate 'a fair settlement' (Nixon, 1978, p. 733). In January 1973 an agreement was concluded at Paris which established a cease-fire and allowed American withdrawal disguised as 'peace with honor'. By 1 April 1973, the only American soldiers serving in South Vietnam were the marines guarding the American embassy in Saigon.

In reality, a humiliated United States had abandoned South Vietnam. Despite the expenditure of billions of dollars and the loss of 58,000 American lives and more than 150,000 wounded, successive presidents from Eisenhower to Nixon had failed to create a bulwark of anti-communism in the South. Without the continuing military, financial and political support of the United States, South Vietnam could not survive as an independent country. This was demonstrated to the world on 30 April 1975 when North Vietnamese troops seized Saigon and brought an end to the Second Indochina War by forcibly uniting the two Vietnams. To perpetuate the memory of Ho, who had died in 1969, Saigon was renamed Ho Chi Minh City in tribute to the man who had for so long led and inspired the struggle for national liberation and unification.

The Vietnamese domino had fallen to the communists, but it did not lead to the establishment of similar regimes throughout Asia and the Pacific. In fact, the struggle for hegemony in Indochina was soon renewed, because the new Socialist Republic of Vietnam (SRVN) sought to emulate the French and include Laos and Cambodia (Kampuchea) within its sphere of influence. This resulted in the dispatch of Vietnamese troops to Cambodia in 1978, an action which prompted the brief retaliatory invasion of northern Vietnam by China in 1979. 'We consider it necessary to put a restraint on the wild ambitions of the Vietnamese and to give them an appropriate lesson', declared the Chinese leader, Deng Xiaoping (Brzezinski, 1983, p. 409). The evidence of deep-seated hostility between China and North Vietnam indicated that American policy had been mistaken in automatically regarding the North Vietnamese as communist puppets. In retrospect, it appeared that American military intervention had greatly intensified the fighting and prolonged what was essentially a local conflict for political ascendancy in Indochina. As George Kennan observed, the Vietnam War had proved to be 'the most disastrous of all America's undertakings over the whole two hundred years of its history' (Moss, 1990, p. 372).

4

Revolution in the Third World

The United Nations

As World War II drew to its close it was natural that the leaders of the Big Three should wish to continue their wartime cooperation into the postwar world. Churchill and Stalin thought in terms of a traditional concert of great powers who would rule and divide the world among themselves. Roosevelt's views were initially similar, but he eventually gave his support to the formation of an international organization of equal sovereign states to ensure the maintenance of peace. In conferences at Dumbarton Oaks in Washington and at San Francisco, American diplomats took the initiative and proposed what amounted to an expanded version of the Old League of Nations. 'We must provide the machinery', stated President Truman in April 1945, 'which will make future peace, not only possible, but certain' (Schlesinger, 1983, V, p. 28). The new body was called the United Nations Organization and membership was open to all independent countries. The name 'United Nations' had been the official title of the Grand Alliance during the war and aptly conveyed the sense of a common endeavour to promote world democracy and cooperation.

The idealist concept was soon undermined by the realities of power politics. While Americans were enthusiastic, the Soviets were suspicious of an organization too much resembling a Western parliament and likely to be dominated by the West. In order to ensure Soviet membership, various concessions were necessary. The most significant was the superior executive role accorded to the Security Council and the granting of the power of veto to its five permanent members. This placed Britain, China, France, the Soviet Union and the United States in a privileged position compared to the ordinary members who formed the General Assembly. By using its veto, any one of the great powers could prevent the United Nations taking a decision which that power considered detrimental to its national interest. Conversely, effective action depended upon the cooperation and goodwill of the permanent members.

Soviet misgivings were justified because the organization was indeed dominated by the Western powers, especially the United States. Symbolic of this was the location of the United Nation's headquarters in New York. Of the initial 51 members, only five were from communist countries. The large number of Latin American nations generally supported the United States. Similarly, most of the Commonwealth countries invariably voted with Britain. The West could therefore expect a large majority in both the Security Council and the General Assembly. Moreover, American influence was further heightened by the fact that the United States provided a substantial amount of the funds for agencies such as the United Nations Relief and Rehabilitation Administration (UNRRA) and possessed a virtual controlling interest in adjunct economic institutions such as the International Monetary Fund (IMF) and the International Bank for Reconstruction and Development (IBRD or World Bank).

The conflict of interests between West and East surfaced at the very first meetings of the United Nations in 1946 when controversy erupted over the admission of Argentina and Poland. Despite Soviet criticism of Argentina's fascist government, Argentine membership was accepted, while the Polish application was temporarily deferred. The Soviets were further disconcerted by Iran's request that the Security Council investigate the Soviet occupation of Azerbaijan. What had been intended as a forum for discussion and negotiation became an arena for confrontation between the great powers. Since the West would invariably win any vote, the Soviet Union resorted to the frequent use of the veto. Between 1946 and 1969 the Soviets issued 105 vetoes. 'The veto is a means of self-defense', explained the Soviet Representative, Andrei Vishinsky (Dallin, 1962, p. 51). Soviet displeasure even extended to a boycott of the Security Council for six months in 1950 as a protest against the refusal to admit Communist China.

The role of the United Nations in responding to international crises threatening world peace was severely constrained by the lack of independent military forces under its control and the use of the veto power in the Security Council. On occasion, the great powers agreed that the United Nations could serve a useful peace keeping function, as in Palestine or Kashmir, and member states were asked to contribute troops and military equipment for this purpose. However, as the Korean War and the Congo (Zaire) crisis in 1960 demonstrated, far from prompting a spirit of compromise, the raising of Cold War issues at the United Nations provoked only bitter and sterile debates. A notable change occurred during the late 1950s when the agenda of subjects under discussion was significantly broadened. The dissolution of the European colonial empires meant that a large number of newly independent nations was created, so that the original membership of the United Nations had almost doubled by 1960. Moreover, a majority of the members now belonged to Africa and Asia. The balance of voting power accordingly shifted against the West. This was demonstrated by the desire of the new nations in the General Assembly to pass resolutions condemning French policy in North Africa and the violation of human rights in South Africa.

As a nation which had won its own independence from colonial rule, the United States was a long-standing champion of self-determination. During World War II, Roosevelt had frequently clashed with Churchill over colonial questions. In the president's opinion, more than a billion 'brown people' resented being ruled by a handful of whites. 'Our goal must be to help them achieve independence', he said in March 1945 (Thorne, 1978, p. 594). The Truman administration upheld the rights of small nations in the United Nations and put diplomatic pressure on Britain and Holland to grant independence to India and Indonesia. But the United States was also the ally and associate of the Western European powers. Its financial support for France in the war against the Vietminh in Indochina demonstrated that strategic interests outweighed anti-colonial sentiment. Moreover, American diplomats represented the world's leading capitalist nation and appeared uncomfortable when confronted with revolutionary political change. Citing the example of disturbances in Indonesia, Acheson noted that independence from colonial rule was not an end, but 'a beginning of new troubles as tragic and bloody as any experience in the past' (Acheson, 1970, p. 331). It was not surprising that many of the new countries should be suspicious of the United States and would liken American 'imperialism' to European colonialism.

While firmly resisting political reform in Eastern Europe, the Soviet Union sought to promote radical change in the wider world by exploiting anti-Western nationalism in Africa and Asia. Amid a fanfare of publicity, Khrushchev and Bulganin initiated the new policy by visiting India, Burma and Afghanistan in 1955. A programme of foreign aid was unveiled and close relations were subsequently cultivated with influential countries such as India and Egypt. Soviet officials pledged their support for 'wars of national liberation' against the Western 'imperialists' and 'warmongers'. These ideas were forcefully expressed in a speech delivered by Khrushchev in 1961:

> The national-liberation movement is an anti-imperialist movement. With the collapse of the colonial system, imperialism has become considerably weaker. Vast territories and enormous masses of people have ceased or are ceasing to serve as a reserve for it, as a source of cheap raw materials and cannon fodder. With the support of the socialist states and all international progressive forces, the Asian, African and Latin American countries are more and more frequently inflicting defeats on the imperialist powers and coalitions. (Schlesinger, 1983, II, p. 659)

The United States responded by increasing its foreign assistance to neutral countries such as India, Indonesia and Yugoslavia. But the American Congress invariably sought to tie aid with political and military strings. The Soviets deliberately adopted a more even-handed posture. Not tainted by links with the former colonial masters, Soviet policy appeared more disinterested and sympathetic.

For ideological and practical reasons, communism possessed many attractions for the new states. The example of the Chinese revolution was particularly pertinent. But the most relevant and appealing model of international behaviour was provided by India. After gaining independence from Britain in 1947, India remained attached to the British Commonwealth, but insisted on pursuing an independent foreign policy. By refusing to choose between East and West, India assumed the role of leader of the 'Third World'. This approach to world politics was also described as 'neutralism' or 'non-alignment'. Its popularity was demonstrated in 1955 when 29 neutral countries attended the Bandung conference in Indonesia. A second meeting was held at Belgrade in 1961. A new bloc of nations emerged which found the problems of economic development more compelling than the politics of the Cold War. They feared external interference in their affairs and sought to avoid this by not becoming embroiled in the conflicts between the superpowers.

Despite a basic lack of financial and military power, the nations of the Third World found strength in their common sense of identity and their increasing numbers. They soon discovered that their majority in the General Assembly of the United Nations could have an impact on international affairs. In the process, they revitalized the economic and cultural agencies of the United Nations. On political issues, the battle against colonialism naturally absorbed the attention of the new members. But their strident attacks upon the ex-colonial masters brought the Third World into a tactical alliance with the communist nations and thereby fixed an anti-Western bias upon neutralism. For example, the admission of 16 new African states in 1960 and Khrushchev's presence at the opening session of the Fifteenth General Assembly occasioned the formulation of Resolution 1514, which affirmed that 'an end must be put to colonialism and all practices of segregation and discrimination associated therewith' (Schlesinger, 1983, V, p. 476). There were 90 votes cast in favour of the resolution, with none against. The eight nations which abstained included the United States, Britain, France, Portugal and South Africa.

The vote on Resolution 1514 demonstrated that the era of Western domination of the United Nations was over. From the point of view of the United States, the United Nations had become an unwelcome forum for demagoguery and anti-Western propaganda. The wheel had turned full circle. During the late 1940s, the Soviet Union had sought to detach itself from the United Nations. But with the notable exception of the crisis in the Congo, it was the United States that pursued a strategy of disengagement from the 1960s onward. The founders of the United Nations had envisaged an instrument to preserve world peace. But the conflict of interests between the great powers ensured that the United Nations was effectively deprived of real power for as long as the Cold War existed. It became therefore primarily an institution to distribute economic and cultural welfare and a platform for the expression of political propaganda. UN troops continued to perform a valuable peace keeping function, especially in the Middle East and Africa. When it came to substantive discussions on Cold War issues, the superpowers preferred to ignore the United Nations and deal directly between themselves. The state of virtual stalemate continued until the late 1980s, when cooperation between the United States and the Soviet Union enabled the United Nations, under American leadership, to undertake a series of military interventions to maintain world peace. The most notable action was the Persian Gulf War in 1991 to punish Iraq for its invasion and annexation of oil-rich Kuwait in August 1990. The territorial ambitions of Iraq's leader, Saddam Hussein, threatened Western rather than Soviet strategic and economic interests in the Persian Gulf. Nevertheless, the leading world powers met in the Security Council and agreed to impose economic sanctions upon Iraq and to pass UN Security Council Resolution 678, which authorised 'all necessary means' to compel Iraqi withdrawal from Kuwait. In so doing, they affirmed the validity of the concept of collective security to maintain and preserve world peace that had led to the creation of the United Nations at the end of World War II.

The Middle East

Stretching from the Indian Ocean to the Mediterranean via the Red Sea, the Middle East has long provided the gateway between Asia and Europe. During the nineteenth century, its strategic and economic value made it an area of contentious international rivalry between Britain, France and Russia. This importance was enhanced by the opening of the Suez Canal in 1869 and the discovery and development in the twentieth century of vast oilfields. Foreign penetration was aided by Arab disunity and the political instability arising from the slow decline of the Ottoman empire. An additional source of tension was the emergence of bitter hostility between Arabs and Jews resulting from the creation of the state of Israel in 1948.

At the close of World War II Britain was regarded as the dominant foreign power in the Middle East. It was soon apparent, however, that British economic and military resources were overextended. By 1948 Britain had evacuated Palestine and was under pressure from Egypt to withdraw from its military base in the

Suez Canal Zone. Historically, the United States had shown marginal interest in the Middle East, but officials in the Truman administration were alarmed that British weakness would encourage Soviet expansion. Consequently, Stalin's diplomatic demands on Turkey to negotiate a defence treaty in 1946 and the maintenance of Soviet troops in northern Iran were viewed with grave suspicion in Washington. 'In picking the Straits and Iran as points of pressure,' noted Secretary of State Dean Acheson, 'they (the Soviets) followed the route of invasion by barbarians against classical Greece and Rome and later of the czars to warm water' (Acheson, 1970, p. 197). To counter the perceived Soviet threat, the Truman administration broke with American diplomatic tradition and became actively involved in the affairs of the Middle East. The politics of the Cold War were therefore thrust upon the region. 'Should we fail to aid Greece and Turkey in this fateful hour,' warned Truman in March 1947, 'the effect will be far reaching to the West as well as to the East' (Schlesinger, 1983, I, p.114).

Preoccupied with domestic reconstruction, Stalin preferred to avoid a confrontation with the United States over the Middle East. Although the sense of urgency was removed, American officials continued to remain vigilant. 'The Arab states', remarked the State Department in 1949, 'presently represent a highly vulnerable area for Soviet exploitation' (Leffler, 1992, p. 287). In terms of strategic priority, the region was ranked ahead of the Far East and second only to Europe, an importance which would later be underlined by the stationing of the powerful American Sixth Fleet in the Mediterranean. Special attention was paid to developing friendly diplomatic relations with oil-rich Saudi Arabia and Iran. Much more controversial, however, was the decision of the Truman administration to recognize the state of Israel only ten minutes after that country's declaration of independence on 14 May 1948. 'There's no Arab vote in America but there's a heavy Jewish vote and the Americans are always having elections', explained the British prime minister, Clement Attlee (LaFeber, 1976, p. 79). The subsequent development of a 'special' relationship between the United States and Israel aroused Arab hostility and undermined American efforts to pursue an even-handed policy in the region.

American diplomats cooperated with their British and French allies to maintain peace and contain Soviet expansion. Fearing the outbreak of an arms race between the Arabs and Israelis, the three Western powers joined together in 1950 to issue the Tripartite Declaration, which attempted to restrict sales of military equipment. There were also discussions to establish a regional security arrangement similar to NATO. British proposals for a Middle Eastern Defence Organization (MEDO) foundered, however, on Egyptian opposition to a continued Western military presence in the Suez Canal Zone. Although MEDO never actually came into being, a small regional grouping was eventually formed by Britain in 1955. It was initially known as the Baghdad Pact and later renamed the Central Treaty Organization (CENTO). The only Arab member was Iraq.

The role of Egypt was crucial. Under the leadership of Gamal Abdel Nasser, the country sought to present a successful model of revolutionary nationalism. One of Nasser's immediate aims was the restoration of full Egyptian sovereignty over the Suez Canal Zone. As he battled against foreign 'imperialism', Nasser became a champion for Pan-Arab unity and a leading figure in the Third World. The governments of Britain and France were alarmed. Fearing the spread of further unrest in their colonies, they adopted a hostile attitude towards Nasser. Moreover, their dependence on supplies of oil from the Middle East made the Suez Canal a matter of vital national importance. The United States, however, was able to take a more sympathetic view of Arab nationalism in keeping with its own anti-colonialist tradition. The Eisenhower administration also wished to prevent Nasser from turning to the Soviet Union for support. American officials therefore looked with favour on Egypt's attempts to introduce economic reform and undertook to give financial assistance to the massive Aswan Dam irrigation project.

Dealing with Third World leaders, however, proved far from easy. A particular dilemma for the United States arose over Nasser's request for arms. The desire to befriend the Egyptian leader had to be measured against the certainty that the weapons would be used against Israel. By insisting upon cash payment, the State Department believed that it had tactfully frustrated Nasser's plans. To the consternation of American officials, Nasser negotiated a trade deal with the Soviet Union in which the latter accepted Egyptian cotton as payment for weapons delivered from Czechoslovakia. When Egypt established diplomatic relations with the government of Red China in May 1956, Dulles was irate. In July the Americans demonstrated their displeasure by withdrawing their pledge of financial support for the Aswan Dam.

A week later Nasser again totally confounded American calculations by announcing the nationalization of the company that controlled and operated the Suez Canal. The governments of Britain and France protested on behalf of their citizens, who were the principal shareholders. After three months of desultory negotiations, hostilities erupted in late October 1956. British and French forces seized the canal, while Israel simultaneously launched an offensive from the east. Eisenhower considered that military intervention was 'a terrible mistake' (Ambrose, 1984, p. 365). He was critical of Nasser, but believed that Egypt's action was legally correct. The United States would not endorse the use of force and proceeded to apply economic pressure on Britain and France to terminate their invasion. Beset by financial and political crisis, the governments of Britain and France reluctantly accepted an American plan for a cease-fire to be implemented by the United Nations.

Eisenhower's desire to bring a speedy end to the conflict was also motivated by his constant anxiety that the Soviet Union would 'make mischief' (Ambrose, 1984, p. 338). However moral and statesmanlike the president's approach, its immediate results were disastrous for the West. Britain and France were publicly humiliated, while Israel was angered at having to give up its conquest of the Gaza Strip. On the other hand, Egyptian control of the canal was reinstated and Nasser was acclaimed as a hero throughout the Arab world. Moreover, Khrushchev gratefully seized the opportunity to divert attention from Soviet repression of the rebellion which was currently taking place in Hungary. He boasted to the international press that his threats to fire missiles at London had compelled the British and French to withdraw. As a sign of the new relationship between Moscow and Cairo, Khrushchev stated that the Soviets would finance the Aswan Dam.

The Suez crisis therefore divided the Western powers, enhanced the reputation of Nasser, and stimulated the rise of Soviet influence in the Arab world. It also marked the replacement of Britain by the United States as the leading Western power in the region. The change was signalled by Eisenhower in a speech on 5 January 1957 outlining what would become known as the 'Eisenhower Doctrine'. He stated categorically that America supported 'without reservation the full sovereignty and independence of each and every nation of the Middle East'. Pointing out the danger to the region posed by communism, he asked for congressional authority to use 'the armed forces of the United States' to assist those countries that requested aid 'against overt armed aggression from any nation controlled by international communism' (Schlesinger, 1983, V, pp. 408–12).

Like Monroe in 1823 and Truman in 1947, Eisenhower unilaterally declared that the United States would protect substantial parts of the globe against a political danger which it alone defined. Predictably, the Soviet Union condemned Eisenhower's 'crude threat to employ force' (Schlesinger, 1983, II, p. 581). But the Cold War perspective was highly misleading. The actions of the superpowers were not responsible for the political turbulence of the Middle East. The ruling Arab elites resented foreign interference, but they were much more concerned with the threat of revolutionary change and Egyptian hegemony implicit in Nasser's Pan-Arab movement. Right-wing regimes such as Lebanon, Jordan and Saudi Arabia welcomed the Eisenhower Doctrine, which they correctly interpreted as seeking to maintain the status quo.

Nasser retaliated by condemning American meddling. He found it easy to whip up anti-American sentiment by making scathing reference to the 'special' relationship existing between the United States and Israel. Egypt and its allies in Syria and Iraq looked to the Soviet Union for military and financial assistance. Khrushchev was only too keen to comply. Such requests suited perfectly his strategy of undermining the West by backing national liberation movements in the Third World. The United States responded by expanding its aid programmes to governments which it considered friendly. But the nations of the Middle East were not transformed into satellites of the superpowers. Indeed, Arab nationalism was not always compatible with Soviet communism. When Nasser arrested Egyptian communists in 1959, Khrushchev described the Egyptian leader as a 'young hothead' (Dallin, 1962, p.125). Moreover, increasing oil revenues gave the Arab states not only a greater sense of independence and self-esteem, but also the financial resources to prepare for war against Israel. While the United States and the Soviet Union were willing to supply the weapons, they did not provide the motivation for the Arab–Israeli struggle. With the exception of the brief American military intervention to support the government of Lebanon in 1958, both superpowers were careful not to become active participants in the succession of internal crises that affected the region.

Africa

After the Portuguese voyages of discovery in the fifteenth century, Sub-Saharan Africa experienced a succession of European invaders 'scrambling' for slaves, trade and territorial dominion. By the middle of the twentieth century, Britain, France and Portugal possessed the largest colonial empires, with a Belgian outpost in the Congo. Despite its size and large population, Sub-Saharan Africa remained the 'dark' continent to the rest of the world. The European powers jealously guarded their colonies and kept them out of the mainstream of international politics.

For the two superpowers, Sub-Saharan Africa was a remote and scarcely known area to which they had traditionally assigned a low strategic priority. The United States had shown a particular interest in developing Liberia as a homeland for ex-slaves, but had maintained relatively modest political and economic contact with the rest of the continent. In accordance with their universal principles, American diplomats advocated an end to colonial rule. On the other hand, they generally subscribed to the racist view prevailing in the West that the vast majority of black Africans had barely emerged from the Stone Age and were not ready for self-government. 'The United States Government has always maintained', stated Assistant Secretary of State George McGhee in 1951, 'that premature independence for primitive uneducated peoples can do them more harm than good' (Schlesinger, 1983, V, p. 552).

Moreover, the colonial powers were also America's closest allies and were extremely sensitive to external interference from whatever source. Consequently, American officials preferred not to encroach on what was a well-established European sphere of influence. Indeed, in contrast to other parts of the globe, Sub-Saharan Africa exhibited remarkable political stability in the years immediately following the close of World War II. However distasteful it was in principle, American officials acknowledged that European colonial rule made the continent safe from communist infiltration. 'In these troubled times', observed McGhee, 'it is gratifying to be able to single out a region of 10 million square miles in which no significant inroads have been made by communism, and to be able to characterize the area as relatively stable and secure' (Schlesinger, 1983, V, p. 549).

The deceptive calm was shattered from the late 1950s onwards as the process of decolonization gathered momentum. Starting with Ghana in 1957, most of Africa was liberated from European rule within less than a decade. The new states identified with the nations of the Third World and sought to adopt a neutral stance in international affairs. There was also considerable support for an exclusive Pan-African grouping, which ultimately found expression in the formation of the Organization of African Unity (OAU) in 1963. The 32 original members, however, were united in name only. Drawn from North, West, Central and East Africa, the OAU presented a panorama of ethnic diversity. Political differences were exacerbated by cultural barriers. Although the members professed non-alignment in international affairs, economic weakness and dependence on the export of staple commodities meant that most countries remained closely tied to the economies of their former colonial rulers. One means of escaping from this state of dependency was to cultivate relations with the superpowers. But the United States and the Soviet Union responded cautiously. So long as there was no major disturbance affecting their national interests, they regarded Africa as an area of minor strategic significance.

It was the crisis in the Congo (Zaire) that thrust Africa temporarily into the centre of Cold War politics. This huge country was granted independence by Belgium on 30 June 1960, but few preparations had been made for the transition from colonial rule to self-government. Almost immediately there were reports of violent disorder. On 5 July the army mutinied and chaos ensued. The copper-rich southern province of Katanga attempted to secede under the leadership of Moise Tshombe. The Congolese prime minister, Patrice Lumumba, appealed to the United Nations for assistance to restore order. Prompted by the UN secretary general, Dag Hammarskjold, the Security Council agreed to dispatch a peace keeping force. American transport planes were made available to airlift UN troops into Leopoldville (Kinshasa). On 15 July the first detachments arrived out of a force which would eventually number 20,000. The largest contingents were initially drawn from Morocco, Tunisia and Ethiopia.

Lumumba also travelled to Washington to solicit military aid. The Eisenhower administration was suspicious of his left-wing views and considered him 'an individual whom it was impossible to deal with' (Ambrose, 1984, p. 586). Rebuffed in the United States, Lumumba turned to the Soviet Union. Khrushchev offered support and proceeded to send 'technicians' and military equipment to the Congo. The Soviet leader justified his action by alleging that the Western powers were colluding with Hammarskjold to destroy Congolese independence. When Lumumba accused the UN peace keeping force of openly sympathizing with his political rivals, American officials believed that a communist coup was imminent. Their policy was to back the United Nations to the hilt. 'We believe that the only way to keep the cold war out of the Congo is to keep the United Nations in the Congo', summed up Adlai Stevenson, the American Representative at the United Nations (Schlesinger, 1983, V, p. 901).

Although the pattern of political events in the Congo was confused, the outcome appeared to vindicate American strategy. In September 1960 Lumumba fell from power, and he was murdered four months later. American complicity was suspected, but never substantiated. Whatever the reasons for his death, the event signalled a set-back for Soviet influence. Soviet technicians proved ill suited to Africa and were soon required to leave the Congo. Largely financed and equipped by the United States, the UN peace keeping force was instrumental in restoring public order and allowing pro-Western Congolese leaders to gain political control. President Kennedy also gave his full support to the military actions which defeated the attempted secession of Katanga. For the United Nations, it was a controversial and expensive military operation which so provoked Khrushchev's fury that the whole future of the organization was called into question. Much to American relief, the Soviet leader preferred diplomatic bluster to a military confrontation in the heart of Africa.

Wishing to keep Cold War politics out of their continent, the majority of African nations approved Kennedy's desire that the crisis in the Congo be resolved by the United Nations. They were also pleased by the president's personal interest in their affairs. Indeed, he was already famous for his speech delivered to the American Senate in 1957 in which he had criticized French repression of Algerian nationalism. Kennedy was also regarded as a sincere supporter of black civil rights in the United States. One of his first acts on becoming president in 1961 was to appoint G. Mennen Williams to the newly created post of assistant secretary of state for African affairs. To illustrate the new importance attached by the United States to Africa, Williams frequently reminded audiences of an important part of the president's inaugural address: 'To those people in the huts and villages of half the globe struggling to break the bonds of mass misery we pledge our best efforts to help them help themselves, for whatever period is required - not because the Communists may be doing it, not because we seek their votes but because it is right' (Schlesinger, 1983, V, p. 638).

With prompting from Kennedy, American economic aid to Africa rose from $100 million in 1958 to almost $380 million in 1962. Although the increase looked impressive, the amount for 1962 represented no more than 11 per cent of total American aid to developing countries. The reality was that American priorities lay in Europe and, especially, in Southeast Asia. It was also acknowledged that Western European governments had more experience of Africa and were better qualified to mount effective aid programmes. 'We shouldn't play "Mr. Big" in every African capital', advised Secretary of State Dean Rusk (Lyons, 1994, p. 248). Moreover, American political and public interest in Africa diminished sharply after Kennedy's death in 1963. The frequent changes of government, often by violent military coups, also tarnished the continent's image in the United States. Criticism emerged in Congress that American aid for such projects as the Volta Dam in Ghana was misguidedly giving support to repressive regimes. However rich Africa might potentially be in raw materials and minerals, it was relatively insignificant in terms of global trade and investment. American business directed most of its interest and investment not to the needy nations of black Africa, but to the affluent, white-ruled republic of South Africa.

The Soviet Union condemned the United States for maintaining close relations with South Africa. Resolutions critical of South Africa's continued presence in Namibia and its racially segregationist policy of apartheid were regularly debated in the General Assembly of the United Nations and proved embarrassing to the United States. Yet Soviet influence in Sub-Saharan Africa did not markedly increase. Indeed, humiliating reverses were suffered when Soviet missions were expelled from the Congo in 1960 and from

Guinea during the following year. In addition, the Soviets faced competition from the Red Chinese, who established a foothold in East Africa. American officials believed that the communists were too officious and aggressive. In 1963 Mennen Williams observed that 'the Communists have to date failed to subvert or capture any African country as a satellite' (Schlesinger, 1983, V, p. 823). After several generations of foreign rule, the new African states were determined to remain free. Non-alignment was the preferred policy to adopt in world affairs. So long as their continent lacked vital economic and strategic significance for the superpowers, the African nations could remain relatively detached from the Cold War.

Latin America

For almost three centuries Spain and Portugal enforced international isolation upon their colonies in the New World. At the beginning of the nineteenth century the Latin American countries, with the principal exception of Cuba, won their independence, but they lacked the power to become a force in world affairs. Indeed, there seemed to be so many changes of government during the nineteenth century that the region acquired a lasting reputation for political disorder and economic mismanagement. European reconquest was prevented, however, by the ability of the new nations to defend themselves and the proprietary interest shown by the United States in its 'sister' republics. In 1823 President James Monroe declared what amounted to a warning to European powers not to meddle in the political affairs of Latin America. The statement evolved into the Monroe Doctrine and its impact was steadily reinforced by America's remarkable political, economic and military development. The European powers came to recognize that American pre-eminence in the western hemisphere not only was a reality, but also provided an invaluable force for stability in what was regarded as a remote and unruly region of the world.

A complicated relationship existed between the United States and the Latin American nations. Although they resided in the same hemisphere, the two peoples were divided by ethnic, linguistic and religious differences. Latin Americans admired the achievements of the great northern republic. But they also resented their growing subordination to the 'Yankees'. Most of all they deplored American military intervention in the countries of the Caribbean area, such as Cuba, Nicaragua and Panama. However, the Latin American nations were too weak and divided among themselves to challenge the supremacy of the United States. During the economic depression of the 1930s, they welcomed American economic assistance and responded warmly to President Franklin D. Roosevelt's declaration that his country would act as a 'good neighbor'. Pan-American solidarity was also strengthened by the threat of fascist aggression from Europe. The United States took the lead in organizing hemispheric defence and persuaded the majority of the Latin American countries to join World War II. The war effort itself was financed and administered from Washington. The Latin Americans mainly supplied raw materials and military bases. While the economic benefits were considerable, their dependence upon the United States noticeably increased. At the same time, the traditional economic links with the European powers were correspondingly greatly reduced.

The Latin American governments expected that close cooperation with the United States would continue after the war. Indeed, American assistance was considered vital to promote economic development, which would combat the massive problems of exploding population growth and the rising expectations of a higher standard of living and social justice. During the war, however, it was evident that the United States was becoming more preoccupied with Europe and the Far East. After 1945 the United States abandoned its traditional isolationism and took on world-wide commitments. In the process, a policy of neglect was adopted towards Latin America. Latin Americans complained that there was no Marshall Plan for them and that they had been allocated an inferior status to Western Europe. In reply, American diplomats preached the values of self-help and private enterprise. Secretary of State Marshall explained in 1948:

> My Government is prepared to increase the scale of assistance it has been giving to the economic development of the American republics. But it is beyond the capacity of the United States Government itself to finance more than a small portion of the vast development needed. The capital required through the years must come from private sources, both domestic and foreign. (Schlesinger, 1983, III, pp. 45–6)

While avoiding discussion of economic matters, American officials displayed much keener interest in asserting their country's exclusive political and military leadership of the hemisphere. A regional system of collective security known as the Rio Treaty (the Inter-American Treaty for Reciprocal Assistance) was established in 1947. Article three of the treaty foreshadowed NATO by providing 'that an armed attack by any State against an American State shall be considered as an attack against all the American States' (Schlesinger, 1983, III, p. 31). During the following year, the Organization of American States (OAS) was created in accordance with article 51 of the UN Charter, which allowed member states to enter into separate regional organizations to deal with local security problems. By ensuring that inter-American disputes would be first submitted to the OAS rather than the United Nations, the United States sought to insulate Latin America from outside political influence and interference.

American officials also assumed that the countries of Latin America would play a supportive role in the emerging Cold War against the Soviet Union. On welcoming the Latin American foreign ministers to a conference at Washington in March 1951, President Truman noted that their purpose was 'to work out ways and means by which our united strength may be employed in the struggle for freedom throughout the world' (Schlesinger, 1983, III, pp. 140–1). Although the area was considered secure from external communist aggression, military assistance programmes were developed after 1951 so that the Latin American governments would assume a larger share of the burden of hemispheric defence. 'By doing this we can release thousands of U.S. soldiers for other duty', noted the State Department in 1951 (Schlesinger, 1983, II, p. 176). While outwardly in favour of democratic governments, the United States found it easier to work with authoritarian regimes that shared America's anti-communist ethos. Prominent examples were Fulgencio Batista in Cuba, the Somoza family in Nicaragua, and Alfredo Stroessner in Paraguay.

In the era of McCarthyism, it was not surprising that American officials were disturbed by the rise of revolutionary nationalism in Latin America. The talk of land reform, greater power for labour unions and nationalization of foreign companies was not a new phenomenon and had been associated with the Mexican Revolution earlier in the twentieth century. It was, however, now attributed not to internal forces but to communist infiltration and subversion. This was most marked in Guatemala, where attempts to confiscate land owned by the Boston-based United Fruit Company were seen as instigated by local communists who had infiltrated into influential positions in the government and organized labor. The Eisenhower administration feared that a Soviet satellite would be created in Central America, and placed increasing pressure on the Guatemalan government to remove alleged communists from office. When President Jacobo Arbenz purchased weapons from Czechoslovakia in 1954, Secretary of State Dulles ominously warned that 'international communism is making great efforts to extend its political control to this hemisphere' (Schlesinger, 1983, III, p. 260). Less than three months later, in June 1954, a small army of political exiles equipped and organized in Honduras by the CIA staged a military coup to bring down Arbenz. Dulles claimed that the Guatemalan people had determined events and that the country's future would now be directed by 'loyal' leaders 'who have not treasonably become the agents of an alien despotism which sought to use Guatemala for its own evil ends' (Schlesinger, 1983, III, p. 285).

Although they supported Dulles in public, Latin American governments were dismayed by America's covert use of armed force to overthrow a legally elected government. Moreover, they were disappointed that their cooperative attitude in the Cold War did not result in the expected economic favours from the United States. Indeed, the United States was increasingly seen as a major obstacle to political and economic reform. Not only did American officials give open support to the most brutal dictatorships, but also they were accused of colluding with their huge corporations to plunder the riches of the hemisphere. Anti-American sentiment emerged at its most virulent when a howling mob in Caracas attacked Vice-President Richard Nixon's motorcade on his 'goodwill' tour in 1958.

The Eisenhower administration was taken aback by the depth of anti-American hostility. It quickly decided to try and remedy affairs by significantly increasing the provision of financial aid for the region. This programme would be further expanded in 1961 by President Kennedy in the form of the 'Alliance for Progress', which he described as 'a vast cooperative effort, unparalleled in magnitude and nobility of purpose to satisfy the basic needs of the American people for homes, work and land, health and schools' (Schlesinger,

1983, III, p. 502). The United States agreed to provide $20 billion over a period of ten years for a scheme that represented a belated equivalent to the Marshall Plan and was similarly intended to help contain the advance of communism in a region suffering from extreme poverty and destitution. But the economic goals were too ambitious and, in marked contrast to the success of the Marshall Plan in Western Europe, the results proved to be acutely disappointing. Unemployment in Latin America actually increased during the decade of the 1960s, while annual economic growth remained stuck at 1.5 per cent and was outstripped by the population explosion.

The personal desire and political pressure for more immediate and tangible results in the battle against communism made the use of military power an attractive policy option for American presidents. This was exemplified in the response to the rise to power in Cuba in 1959 of an avowed revolutionary regime under the leadership of Fidel Castro. American officials were initially puzzled as to whether Castro was a communist. They were certainly concerned by his determination to decrease Cuba's economic dependence on the United States and interpreted this as a calculated challenge to American pre-eminence in the hemisphere. Relations grew increasingly bitter when Castro nationalized American banks and signed a trade agreement with the Soviet Union. Eisenhower considered Castro 'a madman' and authorized the CIA to prepare a covert operation to overthrow him (Ambrose, 1984, p. 556). The attempt 'to give Castro the Guatemala treatment' took place after Eisenhower had left office and ended in disastrous failure at the Bay of Pigs in April 1961. In calling for resistance against the invaders Castro appealed directly not to communist ideology but to Cuban nationalism and long-standing anti-American feeling. He urged: 'Forward Cubans! Answer with steel and with fire the barbarians who despise us and want to make us return to slavery' (Quirk, 1993, p. 371).

The United States was humiliated by the set-back, while Castro's prestige was enormously enhanced. Khrushchev pledged support and declared that the Soviet Union 'will not abandon the Cuban people' (Schlesinger, 1983, III, p. 536). Castro replied by affirming his personal adherence to Marxism-Leninism and aligning Cuba with the communist nations. While the rest of Latin America generally applauded Castro's defiant stand against American bullying they watched with dismay as Cuba became a satellite of the

Soviet Union and a base for launching guerrilla operations to overthrow governments on the mainland of Central and South America. Even more alarming was the threat of nuclear war in the hemisphere caused by Khrushchev's attempt to place missiles on the island in 1962. After some initial reluctance, the Latin American nations approved American proposals to expel Cuba from the OAS and to isolate the island politically and economically.

Although the Soviets had successfully established a bridgehead in Cuba, they used the island as a propaganda showpiece and intelligence base rather than a military fortress. No attempt was made to integrate Cuba into the Warsaw Pact or join a Soviet system of world-wide alliances. This cautious policy was explained by the fact that the western hemisphere was a well-established American sphere of influence. By contrast, the Soviet Union was a remote power which had a history of minimal political and economic contact with the region. Only Argentina, Mexico and Uruguay maintained diplomatic relations with Moscow throughout the 1950s. Indeed, the strongly Catholic societies of Latin America had an innate aversion to communism. Much to the relief of the United States, the Cuban example of enacting a socialist revolution was not directly copied elsewhere in the hemisphere during the 1960s. Indeed, the failure of Cuba's attempts to 'export revolution' to the mainland was illustrated by the capture and death of Che Guevara in Bolivia in 1967. The defeat of the guerrillas was also a reflection of the substantial efforts undertaken by the United States to build up Latin American internal security and police forces and provide instruction in counter-insurgency techniques.

American diplomacy preferred to use military assistance programmes and covert operations to contain communism in the hemisphere. To intervene directly with American forces was considered too politically risky and damaging to America's image in Latin America. Consequently, Kennedy instructed the CIA to conceal the role of the American government in the Bay of Pigs operation. On occasion, however, the influence of Cold War politics resulted in unilateral American military intervention. In the same way that he was determined not to 'lose' South Vietnam, President Lyndon Johnson would not allow 'another Cuba' in the hemisphere. When political chaos erupted in the Dominican Republic in April 1965, he dispatched more than 20,000 American troops to restore order. 'The last thing I wanted – and the last thing the

American people wanted – was another Cuba on our doorstep', he explained (Johnson, 1972, p. 198). The intervention aroused heated controversy within the United States. Johnson was accused of exaggerating the communist threat and reacting with excessive military force. On the other hand, American troops were withdrawn from the Dominican Republic within six months and a pro-American president was elected there in 1966. Moreover, the 'success' of the 1965 intervention compensated to some extent for the earlier disaster at the Bay of Pigs. To Latin Americans, however, it was further evidence that they were more likely to be victims than benefactors of Cold War politics.

In 1965 President Johnson called on the American people to assume the role of the world's policeman not only in the Dominican Republic but also in Vietnam. However, the military success achieved in the Caribbean, where American power was overwhelming, was not repeated in distant Southeast Asia. In fact, Johnson's increasing obsession with the Vietnam War prevented him from acknowledging changes in the nature of the Cold War. Since 1945 the two superpowers had dominated international politics. From the mid-1960s onwards, however, the bipolar world gave way to a more diverse international order. The preference of the Third World for non-alignment and national self-assertion was paralleled by the desire of Western Europe, China and Japan to exercise a more active role in world affairs commensurate with their own growing power and sense of importance. The Cold War was not over and would continue so long as an adversarial relationship persisted between the United States and the Soviet Union. But the tone of the verbal battle noticeably softened as both superpowers increasingly talked of seeking *détente* rather than confrontation.

5

Détente

The Formulation of *Détente*

The 1970s were a period of *détente* between the superpowers. The initiative came from the United States and reflected a significant change that had taken place in the global balance of power during the preceding decade. When President Richard Nixon assumed office in 1969, the United States was no longer regarded as indisputably the world's pre-eminent superpower. The Soviet Union had finally closed the 'nuclear gap' and claimed a position of 'parity' in nuclear weapons with the United States. American predominance in international trade and finance was challenged by the remarkable economic rise of West Germany and Japan during the 1960s. An even more public symbol of the relative decline of American power in the world was the Vietnam War, in which President Johnson's decision to escalate the fighting had not only aroused considerable international criticism but also seriously damaged political and social cohesion within the United States. 'By 1969,' lamented Nixon's national security adviser and later secretary of state, Henry Kissinger, 'the War in Vietnam had become a national nightmare that stimulated an attack on our entire postwar foreign policy' (Kissinger, 1979, p. 64). The resulting determination of the Nixon administration to wind down the Vietnam War reflected the recognition that the United States could no longer sustain the burden of containing the expansion of international communism by military means.

In effect, the ambitious containment strategy dating from the Truman Doctrine and NSC-68 was reversed as Nixon and Kissinger proceeded to adjust the aims and conduct of American foreign policy in accordance with their perception of limited national resources and new developments in international relations. At Guam in July 1969 Nixon announced that the United States would maintain existing treaty obligations, but must expect its allies in the Far East 'to assume the primary responsibility of providing the manpower for [their] own defense' (Melanson, 1991, p. 49). The reluctance to commit American ground troops was both an economy measure and an attempt to 'ensure that there would be no more Vietnams in the future' (Nixon, 1978, p. 395). But the 'Nixon Doctrine' was not intended to be defeatist or merely reactive to events. It formed part of what would become a major diplomatic initiative to achieve American national security and world peace. Indeed, Nixon was convinced that these twin goals were best secured by cultivating friendly and cooperative relations with the Soviet Union. In January 1970 he informed the American Congress: 'We are moving with precision and purpose from an era of confrontation to an era of negotiation' (Melanson, 1991, p. 62). Instead of treating the Soviet Union as an implacable adversary, the United States would actively seek a relaxation of tensions or '*détente*'. Moreover, in what became known as the strategy of 'linkage', Nixon and Kissinger planned to influence Soviet international behaviour by offering incentives in the form of preferential access to American trade, finance and technology. Should Soviet compliance not be forthcoming these incentives would be withdrawn.

The concept of *détente* between the superpowers was not strictly a new development and had been associated with Khrushchev's idea of 'peaceful coexistence' during the late 1950s. The idea had similarly been reflected in the aftermath of the Cuban Missile Crisis when Kennedy and Khrushchev had entered into discussions on arms control, resulting in the 1963 Test Ban Treaty. The Johnson administration had also actively pursued *détente*, but preferred to describe it as 'bridge building'. A measure of success was achieved in 1967 by the holding of a summit meeting between President Johnson and Prime Minister Alexei Kosygin at Glassboro, New Jersey. A return visit was scheduled in the Soviet Union for October 1968, but was cancelled by Johnson as a protest against the Soviet military intervention in Czechoslovakia in August 1968. Nixon's suggestion of relaxing tensions between the superpowers represented therefore as much a continuity as a break with the immediate past. The new Soviet leadership, headed by Leonid Brezhnev, felt flattered at being treated at last as an equal of the United States, but was initially suspicious of overtures from an American president whose political career had been that of a staunch anti-communist and 'Cold Warrior'. After holding a series of meetings in Washington with the Soviet ambassador, Anatoly Dobrynin, Kissinger complained that progress towards *détente* was persistently obstructed by Soviet procrastination and 'immobilism'. 'Inconclusive exchanges in 1969', he later observed, 'degenerated into a series of confrontations that lasted through 1970' (Kissinger, 1979, p. 144).

The most significant boost to *détente* emerged not from Washington or Moscow but from the activities of Western European political leaders, most notably Willy Brandt of West Germany. Brandt belonged to a new generation of Western Europeans who rose to high political office during the 1960s and, according to Kissinger, 'had come to take security for granted and saw economic progress as inevitable' (Kissinger, 1979, p. 1274). Although the 'new' Europeans valued the military protection provided by the American 'nuclear umbrella', their growing political and economic self-confidence encouraged a desire to be less subordinate to the United States. They also tended to be critical of American policy in Vietnam and no longer perceived the Soviet Union as an inveterate enemy of the West. Indeed, as de Gaulle had argued, improved relations between Western Europe and the communist bloc would reduce the risk of nuclear war in Europe and lead to mutually advantageous political and commercial benefits. This thinking attracted increasing support in West Germany and was put into effect by Brandt, who was appointed foreign minister in 1966 and later became chancellor, in October 1969. Brandt's policy was given the name of 'Ostpolitik' ('Eastern policy') and stressed 'normalizing' West Germany's relations with the Soviet Union and the countries of Eastern Europe, including East Germany.

Ostpolitik enjoyed dramatic success. The first and most crucial step was for Brandt to open talks with the Soviet Union. Twenty-five years after the end of World War II he symbolically travelled to Moscow in August 1970 to sign a treaty in which both West Germany and the Soviet Union renounced the use of force against each other and affirmed the 'inviolability' of the existing frontiers in Eastern Europe. This led to rapid Polish–German agreement in December 1970 that confirmed West Germany's recognition of the Oder–Neisse line as the border separating Poland and East Germany. The subsequent negotiations for a treaty to establish official diplomatic relations for the first time between West and East Germany proved more difficult and time-consuming. One reason was the hostility of the East German communist leader, Walter Ulbricht. Another factor was the necessity for parallel talks to take place between the four occupying powers – the United States, the Soviet Union, Britain and France – to clarify the legal status of Berlin. In September 1971 the Quadripartite Pact reaffirmed the existing rights of each power in Berlin and declared that transit in the future between West Berlin and West Germany would be unimpeded. Finally, in December 1972 West and East Germany signed a 'Basic Treaty', which provided for increased commercial and cultural exchanges and also included the establishment of diplomatic relations in the form of permanent missions located in each other's capital. During the following year both Germanies were admitted into the United Nations as separate members of the General Assembly.

Brandt's Ostpolitik was successful in 'normalizing' West Germany's diplomatic relations with the East. In the process, however, West Germany formally accepted the partition of Germany into two separate countries and recognized the frontiers imposed upon Central and Eastern Europe by the Red Army in 1945. While this might justifiably be interpreted as a Soviet diplomatic victory, it also significantly contributed to European security by denoting a resolution of the problem of Germany's political structure, an issue which had originally precipitated the collapse of the Grand Alliance and had seemed incapable of solution for over two decades. Moreover, the controversial question of Berlin, which had threatened to erupt into war in 1948, 1958 and 1961, was also evidently settled by a Soviet guarantee of unimpeded transit between West Germany and West Berlin. In effect, the Soviets had withdrawn their traditional insistence that East Germany control the access routes overland to Berlin.

The Nixon administration had been outwardly supportive of Ostpolitik but, as Kissinger remarked, 'without enthusiasm' (Kissinger, 1979, p. 531). This ambivalence was explained by American apprehension that the Soviets would regard Ostpolitik as an opportunity to sidetrack talks with the United States and concentrate instead on pursuing 'selective *détente*' with West Germany. The aim of such a strategy would be to isolate the United States and foment division within the Western alliance. But Brandt constantly stressed the fundamental importance of the Atlantic alliance for West Germany and ensured that Nixon was closely informed of diplomatic developments. American anxieties were also relieved by the fact that Soviet capacity for diplomatic manoeuvre was limited. While the Soviet leadership was gratified by West German recognition of the disputed postwar boundaries, they were also eager for increased economic contact not only with West Germany but also with all the countries of the West and especially the United States. Khrushchev had boasted in 1961 that the Soviet economy would overtake that of the United States during the 1970s. By 1970, however, it was evident that the economies of the Soviet Union and Eastern Europe had fallen considerably behind those of the West. Moreover, economic discontent was growing among the civilian population in the satellite countries, and was held to be responsible for the emergence of the reform movement in Czecho-slovakia in 1968 and the outbreak of riots in Poland in December 1970 which had brought about the overthrow of the Polish communist leader, Wladyslaw Gomulka. Brezhnev was determined not to relinquish Soviet control over Eastern Europe. In 1968 his statement of policy known as the 'Brezhnev Doctrine' had declared that military force would be used to ensure that the establishment of a communist state was irreversible. Nevertheless, he recognized that *détente* offered 'a shortcut to modern technology and capital' (Kissinger, 1979, p. 151), and sought to reverse the restrictive policies of Stalin and Khrushchev that had attempted to develop a closed and self-sufficient communist economic bloc.

Growing difficulties with China also placed the Soviets at a tactical disadvantage in their dealings with the United States. Since 1956 the Soviet Union and China had competed in an increasingly bitter ideological battle for leadership of the world communist movement. A dangerous military dimension was added to the conflict during the 1960s when China claimed sovereignty over large tracts of territory in Central Asia which had been incorporated within imperial Russia during the nineteenth century. The Soviets rejected the Chinese claim to this territory and responded by strengthening their air defences and more than doubling the number of Soviet troops stationed along the 4,000-mile common border. In March 1969 a serious border incident occurred, involving fighting and casualties, between Soviet and Chinese solders on Damanski Island/Zhenbao on the Ussuri River in northeast Asia. The prospect briefly loomed of a Sino-Soviet war possibly involving a Soviet nuclear strike on China. Both governments, however, preferred to defuse the conflict and entered into talks in October 1969, which failed to produce a settlement but meant that the existing borders remained undisturbed.

American diplomats played no active role in the evolving Sino-Soviet conflict. Indeed, the United States had never formally recognized the People's Republic of China and continued to regard Taiwan as the legitimate government of China. In the absence of official relations, diplomatic business was obliquely transacted by third parties or in meetings held at Warsaw between the American and Chinese ambassadors to Poland. These occasions were eventually cancelled by China in 1968 in protest against American bombing of North Vietnam. China, however, indicated in December 1969 that it wanted to reopen the Warsaw talks. 'China's cautious overtures to us', Kissinger believed, 'were caused by the rapid and relentless Soviet military build up in the Far East' (Kissinger, 1979, p. 693). American diplomats were wary because for two decades 'Red' China had been a country dedicated to promoting world revolution and an avowed enemy of the United States. On the other hand, Nixon was receptive to the idea of a *rapprochement* between the two countries because this would allow his diplomatic offensive to evolve into the grander concept of an 'era of negotiation'. He regarded the Chinese as 'a great and vital people who should not remain isolated from the international community' (Nixon, 1978, p. 545). In the shorter term, however, Nixon hoped that an 'opening' to China might materially assist his policy of extricating the United States from the Vietnam War. Moreover, any improvement in American relations with China would create what became popularly known as 'the China card', which could be played by the United States against the Soviets to persuade them to be more conciliatory and responsive to *détente*. Kissinger personally preferred to use the term 'triangular diplomacy' to describe the intersection of the foreign policies of the three countries in which the United States would hold the balance. 'To have the two Communist powers competing for good relations with us could only benefit the cause of peace; it was the essence of triangular strategy', he later remarked (Kissinger, 1979, p. 836).

Events moved rapidly in 1971 after the Chinese government caused an international sensation in April by publicly inviting an American table-tennis team to visit China as soon as it had completed a tournament at the World Table Tennis Championships in Japan. This began a period of 'ping-pong diplomacy' during which Kissinger secretly visited China in July. His trip was appropriately given the code name 'Polo' after Marco Polo, the celebrated traveller of the thirteenth century who had made history by revealing China to the West. Kissinger returned to Washington with tales of Chinese hospitality and an invitation for a presidential visit to Peking (Beijing). An elated Nixon astonished American public opinion and the world by immediately announcing that he intended to go to China and 'seek the normalization of relations' between the two governments. The visit took place in February 1972 and its highpoint was the personal meeting between Nixon and Mao Zedong, the respective champions of capitalism and militant international communism. The American president euphorically described his seven days in Beijing as 'the week that changed the world' (Nixon, 1978, p. 580). Furthermore, the implication that events of great historic importance were taking place was conveyed by the accompanying presence of a plane-load of journalists and television engineers who ensured that public events were televised live in the United States.

With the American presidential election less than a year away, Nixon was undoubtedly intent on making political capital from his visit to China. Nevertheless, he had contributed significantly to a *rapprochement* between the United States and China which effectively ended the Cold War in the Far East. American public opinion was generally enthusiastic about the prospect of 'normalizing' relations, and speedily cast aside two decades of perceiving Red China as the dedicated agent of a monolithic communist conspiracy orchestrated from Moscow. In fact, China now appeared ironically as an invaluable force to contain Soviet expansion in Asia. The gains for China were that Nixon's visit pointed the way to profitable commercial and cultural contacts with the West and Japan. Although controversy over the exact status of Taiwan prevented the establishment of full diplomatic relations between the United States and China, each government agreed to set up its own 'liaison office' in the other's capital. Of more immediate importance to the Chinese was the coded warning to the Soviet Union contained in the Shanghai Communiqué signed by Nixon and the Chinese prime minister, Zhou Enlai, that neither the United States nor China 'should seek hegemony in the Asia Pacific region and each is opposed to efforts by any other country or group of countries to establish such hegemony' (Nixon, 1978, p. 577).

The aim of American diplomacy was not to take sides in the Sino-Soviet conflict, but to seek a relaxation of tensions simultaneously with both communist powers. While Nixon deservedly gained plaudits as a world statesman and peacemaker, there were few tangible gains to emerge from the China visit. Contrary to American hopes, China continued to aid the North Vietnamese, who even felt emboldened to launch a spring offensive in South Vietnam. Indeed, Nixon and Kissinger had always believed that their most important negotiations would be with the Soviet Union. They had even worried that a *rapprochement* with China might anger the Soviets. Events demonstrated, however, that the mere fact that American–Chinese relations were improving had been enough to shock the Soviets and to stimulate them to push for *détente* with the West. 'After the announcement of the President's trip to Peking,' Kissinger remarked with gratification, 'the unsettled issues on Berlin were resolved in one week to our satisfaction' (Kissinger, 1979, pp. 837–8). The Soviets were so eager for Nixon to attend a summit meeting with Brezhnev in Moscow that they even hinted it should take place before his visit to Beijing! Despite their failure to alter Nixon's timetable, the Soviets demonstrated that they wanted to move fast on substantive issues in order to ensure a successful summit meeting when Nixon came to Moscow in May 1972. As Brezhnev later commented, Nixon went 'to Peking for banquets but to Moscow to do business' (Kissinger, 1979, p. 836).

The Moscow Summit

Neither Nixon nor Brezhnev regarded the Moscow summit as the occasion for them personally to enter into complex and time-consuming negotiations. Their main function was to appear as world statesmen at televised ceremonies in which they would affix their signatures to a series of 'protocols' or agreements that had been previously thrashed out over a period of weeks and months by teams of lower-level officials. Certain details in the protocols, however, had remained unresolved and required final approval from Nixon and Brezhnev. The protocols were not, therefore, meaningless exercises in public relations. In fact, they served to advance the process of *détente* by facilitating superpower cooperation over a range of commercial, scientific and cultural activities including space exploration, public health and environmental protection. The agreement which attracted the most attention, however, was the Strategic Arms Limitation Treaty (SALT I) that set limits on the number of nuclear weapons and was described by Nixon as 'the first step towards arms control in the thermonuclear age' (Nixon, 1978, p. 618).

Discussions over disarmament had regularly engaged the superpowers throughout the 1960s and had resulted in the 1963 Test Ban Treaty and the 1968 Non-Proliferation Treaty. These treaties, however, did not prevent the United States and the Soviet Union from continuing to develop and stockpile ever more destructive and sophisticated nuclear weapons. Particular importance was attached to 'strategic' weapons which possessed the long-range capability of striking at an enemy's territory. For example, American military strategy was based upon the capacity to hit targets all over the world with bombs and missiles fired from a triad of powerful land, sea and air forces. In contrast, the Soviets preferred to concentrate on developing large numbers of land-based surface-to-surface (SS) ICBMs. The SS-9, which first appeared in 1967, carried a 25-megaton warhead. This was the equivalent of 25 million tons of TNT and was five times more powerful than its American counterpart, the Titan missile. The building and deployment of such missiles reflected the determination of the Soviets to close the 'nuclear gap' and reverse the strategic inferiority that they believed had placed them at a severe disadvantage during the 1962 Cuban Missile Crisis. 'Thus, inexorably,' noted Kissinger, 'the overwhelming preponderance that we had enjoyed in the Forties and Fifties was being eroded first into equality, eventually into vulnerability, of our land-based forces' (Kissinger, 1979, p. 190). By the late 1960s it was acknowledged in the West that the Soviets had virtually achieved 'nuclear parity' with the United States. In the case of ICBMs they even enjoyed superiority in actual numbers. Estimates for 1969 showed that the Soviets possessed 1,198 ICBMs compared to an American total of 1,054.

A curious feature of the strategic arms race was 'thinking the unthinkable'. This involved military experts and scientists making complex calculations about the 'scenario' of a future war and how much nuclear weaponry was needed not only to absorb a surprise 'first strike' by the enemy, but also to allow retaliation with a 'second strike' that would inflict massive damage upon the aggressor's industry and population. Ironically, the likelihood of nuclear war was reckoned to diminish as each superpower became so powerful that full-scale conflict between them would have been suicidal because it must inevitably have resulted in a global holocaust of MAD. Reassurance that MAD would 'deter' the superpowers from starting a war was undermined, however, by the development of a new weapons system consisting of anti-ballistic missiles (ABMs) that were designed specifically to intercept and destroy incoming enemy missiles. Although it originated as a purely defensive weapon, the ABM theoretically made it feasible for one side to win a nuclear war by launching a surprise first strike in the knowledge that its ABM defences would limit the damage which would be incurred from a retaliatory second strike. The Soviets were first reported to be establishing an ABM system around Moscow during the mid-1960s. The Americans responded with plans to have their own ABM defences in place by the early 1970s.

Both superpowers, however, were reluctant to embark on an escalation of an arms race that was already highly expensive and arguably resulted in less rather than more security. Formal talks to prepare a bilateral treaty specifically halting the build-up of nuclear weapons had begun in 1966, but were postponed as a result of the Soviet invasion of Czechoslovakia in 1968. The election of a new American president in 1968 presented an opportunity for the resumption of negotiations. 'Arms control', noted Kissinger, 'was seen almost universally as an area for a breakthrough' (Kissinger, 1979, p. 131). Indeed, the prospects of success were significantly enhanced by the fact that the Soviets were close to nuclear parity with the United States. It would have been disadvantageous for them to have accepted a curb on nuclear weapons while they were in a position of inferiority and attempting to catch up. On the American side, there was recognition that it was economically and strategically sensible to base future policy on seeking 'sufficiency' rather than 'superiority' in nuclear weapons. 'Absolute superiority in every area of armaments would have been meaningless, because there is a point in arms development at which each action has the capacity to destroy the earth', declared President Nixon (Nixon, 1978, p. 415). He argued that the superpowers should establish an acceptable military balance to reduce the risk of nuclear holocaust.

At Helsinki in November 1969 American and Soviet officials began negotiations under the title of 'Strategic Arms Limitation Talks'. Further sessions took place in Helsinki and Vienna and eventually resulted in the protocols that were signed by Nixon and Brezhnev at the Moscow summit in 1972. The agreement known as SALT I was in two parts and consisted of a treaty relating to defensive capabilities and an 'interim agreement' concerning offensive weapons. The 'ABM Treaty' was to be of unlimited duration and sought to prevent either signatory from fully developing ABMs and thereby gaining a strategic advantage over the other. The main stipulation was to allow each side to deploy no more than two ABM systems, one to protect the national capital and the other a designated ICBM base. The interim agreement sought to 'freeze' the number of land and sea 'launchers' capable of firing offensive nuclear missiles. In effect, one launcher was regarded as the equivalent of a single missile. The agreement was initially to last for five years, during which time it would be subject to renegotiation and eventual renewal. During this period the United States agreed to hold their current number of land-based ICBMs at 1,054 while the Soviets could expand from 1,530 to 1,610. A limit was also placed on submarine-launched ballistic missiles (SLBMs), at 710 for the United States and 950 for the Soviets.

Although the terms of SALT I appeared superficially generous to the Soviets, the balance of strategic power in 1972 actually remained in favour of the United States. The agreement stipulated that there would be fewer American missiles, but these were known to be more accurate than the heavier Soviet rockets. Moreover, the actual significance of numbers was greatly diminished by the technological superiority enjoyed by the United States in the development of multiple independently targetable re-entry vehicles (MIRVs). This meant that a single missile would be equipped with several nuclear warheads, each of which could be aimed to hit a separate target. In addition, the United States was much superior to the Soviet Union in the number and quality of its long-range and fighter bombers.

The lead remained intact because SALT I excluded aircraft. Not only did the United States possess higher-quality weapons but it also maintained a ring of land bases and continuous submarine patrols spanning the globe which allowed it to strike easily at the Soviet Union. By contrast, the Soviet Union was relatively land-locked and, in the event of a war with the United States, its strategy would be dependent on firing long-range ICBMs. Finally, the apparent Soviet advantage in numbers of missiles allowed in SALT I did not take into account the existence of British and French nuclear weapons. Britain and France were not party to the interim agreement although they were allies of the United States. In fact, to the relief of the British and French governments, SALT I actually validated their continued possession of independent nuclear forces.

Implementation of *Détente*

The public proclamations of *détente* brought initial political benefits for both Nixon and Brezhnev. Nixon's historic journeys to Beijing and Moscow enhanced his image as a peacemaker and helped him to secure a landslide victory in the American presidential election of November 1972. In the Soviet Union, Brezhnev's personal ascendancy within the Politburo was further consolidated. An invitation to visit the United States in June 1973 confirmed his growing international status. Particularly pleasing to the Soviet leader was the increase in economic cooperation with the West. The gains from Ostpolitik were already evident and would lead to a quadrupling in Soviet trade with West Germany from 1970 to 1975. The prospects of *détente* with the United States were similarly alluring. In fact, a long-standing barrier to Soviet–American trade had been removed shortly after the Moscow summit when the Soviets approved a settlement to repay debts owed to the United States arising from lend-lease during World War II. In return they received generous credits to finance the purchase of American imports. Most of all, the Soviets desperately needed American grain to rectify shortages caused by a series of bad harvests. Taking advantage of favourable credit terms they quickly bought up the entire American grain surplus at below world prices. Americans later complained of 'the great grain robbery'. 'It must be conceded', admitted Kissinger, 'that the Soviet Union played a cool hand and outwitted us' (Kissinger 1979, p. 1269). Nevertheless, the American economy had much to gain from a boom in trade with the Soviet Union that rose in value from $220 million in 1971 to $2.8 billion in 1978.

The desire to promote *détente* also presented an opportunity to follow up the achievements made by Ostpolitik towards resolving the question of European security. Two parallel conferences involving the superpowers and their allies were started in 1973. The series of meetings, which took place at Vienna, was given the title of Mutual and Balanced Force Reductions (MBFR) and essentially considered ways of reducing the size of conventional military forces located in Central and Eastern Europe. These talks, however, were soon overwhelmed by technical complexities and made little substantive progress. The other conference was held in Helsinki. It was known as the Conference on Security and Cooperation in Europe (CSCE) and its discussions ranged over wider diplomatic, political and cultural matters. In August 1975 an agreement known as the Helsinki Final Act, more popularly referred to as the 'Helsinki Accords', was concluded and signed by 33 European countries plus the United States and Canada. The Helsinki Accords were gratifying to the Soviets because they included, for the first time, not only the formal international recognition of existing borders in Eastern Europe but also a statement that these should not be changed by the use of force. In exchange the Soviets consented to Western pressure for the inclusion of the so-called 'Basket III' provision in which all signatories proclaimed their respect for human rights and political freedoms. The form of words was similar to the Declaration of Liberated Europe made at the Yalta conference in 1945, and was likewise regarded more as a declaration of intent than as a legally binding document. On this occasion, however, a committee was established in Helsinki with the task of reporting on the future progress of Basket III. Much to the annoyance of the Soviet leadership, this committee established 'Helsinki Watch' groups in the Soviet Union and Eastern Europe that, by their very existence, served to encourage political 'dissidence' and to draw public attention to the issue of 'human rights'.

While *détente* undoubtedly promoted cooperation and lessened tensions, the superpowers still remained ideological rivals. '*Détente* was conceived as a relationship between adversaries,' remarked Kissinger, 'it did not pretend friendship' (Kissinger, 1982, p. 469).

The American diplomat acknowledged the pleasing development of a growing personal rapport between Nixon and Brezhnev, but he privately described the latter as 'a convinced Communist who sees politics as a struggle with an ultimate winner' (Kissinger, 1979, p. 242). This was confirmed by Brezhnev's frequent affirmation of the principles of Marxism–Leninism, declaring that the victory of communism was inevitable. While the Soviet leader welcomed *détente*, he reminded the West that 'revolution, the class struggle, and liberation movement cannot be abolished by agreements' (Garthoff, 1994a, p. 47). Kissinger calculated, however, that Soviet expansionism in international affairs, which he preferred to characterize as 'adventurism', could be best moderated by the policy of linkage. But the idea of the United States patronizingly dispensing rewards or penalties to the Soviet Union directly contradicted the underlying principle of *détente* that both countries were to be considered as equals. Not only did Brezhnev refuse to recognize the principle of linkage but Kissinger's implicit assumption of American superiority was belied by America's financial and military weakness, reflected in the fall in the international exchange value of the dollar and the failure to win the Vietnam War. Moreover, while Brezhnev enjoyed unchallenged dominance within the Soviet Politburo, the prestige and authority of Nixon and Kissinger were severely shaken by the political scandal of Watergate and by domestic criticism directed against what was alleged to be the abuse of executive power by the 'imperial presidency'. 'Nixon's capacity to lead collapsed as the result of Watergate', Kissinger regretfully concluded (Kissinger, 1979, p. 741). The image of presidential weakness was reinforced by Nixon's successor, Gerald Ford, who was relatively inexperienced in foreign affairs and lacked an electoral mandate. Ford had not been a candidate in the 1972 presidential election and had been appointed by Nixon to the vice-presidency in 1973.

The domestic political difficulties of the Nixon administration contributed to the failure to conclude a new SALT treaty to replace the 1972 interim agreement, which was due to expire in 1977. The main obstacle to progress on arms control, however, was the evident unwillingness of both superpowers to abandon their arms race with each other. Behind the public advocacy of *détente* and disarmament lay the reality that the freeze on missile numbers in SALT I had never been intended to prevent either side from continuing to develop and modernize its existing weapons. Consequently, much to the alarm of the Soviets, the Americans proceeded to carry out research and development on new weapons, notably air-launched cruise missiles (ALCMs) which could fly low to avoid radar, the Trident nuclear submarine, and a long-range supersonic bomber known as the B-1. The cause of concern on the American side was to learn that the Soviets were developing their own supersonic bomber, called the Backfire, and in 1973 were successfully testing ICBMs with MIRVS. The subsequent development of a Soviet MIRVed SS-18, with each missile capable of carrying up to ten warheads, substantially increased the offensive first-strike capability of the Soviet strategic forces and revived American fears of a 'missile gap'. It also devalued the significance of the fixed numbers originally agreed to in the 1972 agreement. 'The Soviets were using the quantitative freeze to engage in a qualitative race', concluded Kissinger (Kissinger, 1979, p. 1011).

Both superpowers, however, wanted *détente* to continue and regarded the negotiation of a new arms control treaty as an essential element in the process. The main task was to recalculate the freeze on the number of missiles so that it included weapons which had been omitted in 1972. Responding to domestic political pressure, American officials insisted that there must also be numerical equality. The concept of an agreement lasting for ten years and based upon the principle that the final numbers should reflect 'essential equivalence' and 'equal aggregates' was accepted by the time Nixon visited Moscow in 1974 for his third summit meeting with Brezhnev. But further progress was halted by Nixon's dramatic resignation from the presidency in August 1974. The new president, Gerald Ford, retained Kissinger as secretary of state and expressed his desire to continue the talks on arms control. At the Vladivostok summit meeting in November 1974, Ford and Brezhnev approved a draft agreement which was intended to form the basis of a new treaty to be known as SALT II. In contrast to SALT I, the agreement stressed parity by stipulating that each side would be limited to the same number of offensive missiles. This figure was fixed at 2,400, which was approximately the number allowed to the Soviets in 1972. The term 'offensive missile' was replaced by 'strategic nuclear delivery vehicle' because the overall total included, for the first time, MIRVed missiles and long-range bombers. Although the number of MIRVed missiles was set at 1,320 out of the total of 2,400, no limit was placed on the actual number of warheads that a single missile would be equipped with. Conscious that the Soviet SS-18 could have up to ten warheads while the American Minuteman missile was limited to three, critics in the United States argued that the Soviets would possess a superiority in 'throw-weight' of mega-tonnage which placed the relatively weaker American nuclear forces in a 'window of vulnerability' (Talbott, 1989, p. 156). In his campaign to challenge Ford for the Republican presidential nomination in 1976 Ronald Reagan stressed that the terms of the proposed SALT II were far too advantageous to the Soviet Union: 'Under Kissinger and Ford, this nation has become Number Two in a world where it is dangerous – if not fatal – to be second best. All I can see is what other nations the world over see: collapse of the American will and the retreat of American power' (Ford, 1979, p. 373). Ford described Reagan's statements as 'inflammatory and irresponsible', but the domestic debate over the relative merits of the treaty became so contentious that he decided to delay submitting SALT II to the American Senate for ratification until after the 1976 presidential election. Progress on arms control was therefore halted by the dictates of American politics.

Superpower Conflicts in the Third World

The inherent shortcomings of *détente* were most apparent in the heightening rather than the lessening of superpower tensions in the Third World. This was especially the case in the Middle East, where the temptation and opportunity for external interference had been enhanced by the outbreak of the Six-Day war in 1967. Israel's spectacular victory led to large territorial conquests at the expense of Egypt, Syria and Jordan, which, according to President Nixon, were 'so overwhelming that it was inevitable that further wars would be fought by Israel's neighbors for repossession of these conquered and occupied territories' (Nixon, 1978, p. 477). The resulting instability meant that superpower rivalry in the region intensified rather than diminished. As the principal supplier of economic and military aid to Israel, the United States had long been identified as the protector of Israel. The Soviets, who had broken off diplomatic relations with Israel in 1967, supported the Arab nations and 'acted as advocate of the Arab cause' (Kissinger, 1979, p, 347). In essence, however, the policies of the superpowers were motivated by traditional Cold War politics. For example, in language reminiscent of the administrations of Truman and Eisenhower, Nixon explained: 'The Soviets wanted to maintain their presence in the Middle East, not because of ideological support for the cause of Arab unity but because it was through Egypt and the other Arab countries that the Soviets could gain access to what the Russians had always wanted – land, oil, power, and the warm waters of the Mediterranean' (Nixon, 1978, p. 477).

The superpowers actively aided and abetted the arms race between their respective 'client states' in the Middle East. In 1968 the United States sold state-of-the-art F-4 Phantom jet fighters to Israel. The Soviets responded by supplying Egypt with surface-to-air missiles (SAMs) which were designed to shoot down the F-4s. In addition, 20,000 Soviet 'advisers' were sent to Egypt to operate the missiles and help to reorganize the country's military forces. Although Egypt was a non-communist country, Kissinger regarded it to all intents and purposes as 'in effect a Soviet military base' (Kissinger, 1979, p. 1279). This development was underlined in March 1971 when Anwar el-Sadat, who had succeeded to the Egyptian presidency after Nasser's death in September 1970, signed a treaty of friendship and cooperation with the Soviet Union.

Despite their dependence on external military supplies, neither Israel nor Egypt was an obedient satellite of the superpowers. Both countries regarded Cold War politics as a valuable means to an end which they would define for themselves. For Israel, the paramount objective was to ensure national survival and security. The goal of President Sadat was to make Egypt militarily strong enough to renew the armed struggle against Israel and regain the territories lost in 1967. Indeed, in July 1972 Sadat displayed his annoyance at Soviet attempts to withhold military aid by peremptorily ordering a large number of the Soviet advisers in Egypt to leave the country. Sadat's capacity for bold and unexpected action was repeated on 6 October 1973, the Jewish holy day of Yom Kippur, when Egypt and Syria attacked Israel without warning. Taken by surprise, the Israelis were initially forced to retreat before the Egyptian offensive in the Sinai peninsula, but they soon recovered and were able to inflict a heavy defeat on the enemy forces.

Although the United States and the Soviet Union airlifted large supplies of military aid to their respective clients, both superpowers wanted a speedy end to the conflict in case it exploded into a full-scale regional war. Their preferred course was to work together through diplomacy and arrange a cease-fire under the auspices of the Security Council of the United Nations. Such action was very much in the spirit of *détente,* but Nixon queried whether the Soviets possessed an ulterior motive. 'It was hard for me to believe that the Egyptians and the Syrians would have moved without the knowledge of the Soviets, if not without their direct encouragement', he remarked (Nixon, 1978, p. 921). American suspicions of collusion between the Soviet Union and Egypt were heightened when Brezhnev threatened to dispatch Soviet troops to protect Egyptian forces from Israeli attack. The prospect of external military intervention so alarmed officials in Washington that they wondered whether the Soviets were simply bluffing. 'We could not run the risk that they were not', considered Kissinger, and he added: 'If we remained passive in the face of the threat, the Soviet leadership would see no obstacle to turning it into a reality' (Kissinger, 1982, p. 585). On 24 October the Nixon administration issued a state of global alert known as Defence Condition III, which instructed American military forces to go immediately to the highest state of combat readiness in peace time. Despite his advocacy of *détente,* Nixon's perception of American national interest prompted him to replace negotiation with confrontation and cause a dramatic showdown between the superpowers that was comparable in its intensity to the 1962 Cuban Missile Crisis. On 25 October Soviet diplomats acted as if Brezhnev's threat of intervention had never been made. 'The Soviets had backed off', concluded Kissinger (Kissinger, 1982, p. 597). The same day saw an end of the war and acceptance by Israel, Egypt and Syria of a cease-fire to be supervised by the UN.

The firm and decisive policy pursued by Nixon and Kissinger boosted American prestige in the Middle East and resulted in the emergence of the United States as the central peacemaker and mediator in the dispute between Israel and Egypt. This took the form of 'shuttle diplomacy', in which Henry Kissinger virtually commuted for two years between the capitals of the region. Progress was slow, but Kissinger was able to exploit America's special relationship with Israel and his close personal rapport with Sadat to persuade both sides to accept the creation of a buffer zone to separate their respective armies in the Sinai. A comprehensive peace settlement including Israel's military withdrawal from the Sinai and Egypt's recognition of Israel's right to exist as a sovereign nation state eluded Kissinger and did not materialize until 1979. Nevertheless, Kissinger's 'shuttle diplomacy' had been successful in bringing Israel and Egypt together in constructive peace talks. American diplomacy also succeeded in significantly reducing Soviet influence in the region. Kissinger acknowledged that the Soviets had not obstructed his diplomatic activities and attributed this to the mutual desire of both superpowers for peace and *détente*. He was clearly delighted, however, that American policy had contributed to the humiliating setback to Soviet diplomatic ambitions in Egypt, a development that was confirmed in 1976 by Sadat's abrupt and unilateral termination of the 1971 Soviet–Egyptian treaty.

Seeking an alternative client state to Egypt in the Middle East, the Soviets cultivated close relations with Syria and sent increasing amounts of military aid to that country. This effectively undermined the achievements claimed by American diplomacy, because Israel felt more threatened than ever by the implacable hostility of Syria and also by the growing incidence of organized terrorism most often associated with the activities of the Palestine Liberation Organization (PLO). The PLO had been formed in 1964 and was dedicated to the creation of an Arab state in Israeli-occupied Palestine. Moreover, American satisfaction with the outcome of Kissinger's diplomacy was severely shaken by the retaliatory action of the Organization of Petroleum Exporting Countries (OPEC), which included leading oil-producing states of the Middle East such as Saudi Arabia, Iran, Iraq and Libya. Angered by American military support of Israel during the Yom Kippur War, the Arab members of OPEC cut back oil production and briefly placed an embargo on exports to the United States in 1973–4. The result was a dramatic increase in the price of crude oil, from $2 to $8 a barrel. The ensuing 'oil shock' and related 'energy crisis' plunged the world economy into recession for much of the 1970s. In the United States, the public was bewildered to find itself so vulnerable to external economic forces. The suspicion that the Soviet Union was implicated in persuading OPEC to push up the price of oil contributed to the growing disillusionment in the United States over *détente*.

American concern was also aroused by the marked increase of Soviet activities in Sub-Saharan Africa. During the 1970s the Soviets chose to become actively involved in a region which both superpowers had tended to neglect ever since the 1960 Congo Crisis. The revival of interest reflected the Soviet pursuit of their traditional policy of promoting the class struggle and encouraging movements for 'national liberation' in the Third World. In addition, Africa was assigned a greater strategic importance as a result of the development of Soviet military power, especially a powerful navy with the capacity to undertake global missions. An example of the 'projection' of Soviet power was illustrated in Angola, a country that had become formally independent from Portugal in 1975. Although the three principal factions which fought for political dominance in Angola were motivated largely by internal political and tribal factors, they could not avoid becoming entangled in Cold War politics. For ideological reasons the Soviets favoured the Marxist Popular Movement for the Liberation of Angola (MPLA). A smaller organization, the National Front for the Liberation of Angola (FNLA), was opposed to the MPLA and, consequently, attracted support initially from China and also secret funding from the United States. The powerful neighbouring state of South Africa openly backed the National Union for the Total Independence of Angola (UNITA). Responding to the outbreak of civil war in 1975, the Soviets airlifted weapons and speedily transported more than 20,000 Cuban troops to support the MPLA. The use of Cubans to act as a proxy force for Soviet troops alarmed the Ford administration. 'Angola represents the first time that the Soviets have moved militarily at long distance to impose a regime of their choice', noted Kissinger in 1976 (Garthoff, 1994a, p. 580). Despite Kissinger's warnings of the global threat posed by Soviet 'adventurism', the American Congress proved unwilling to vote funds to aid the opponents of the MPLA. Mindful of the so-called 'Vietnam syndrome', American congressmen feared that the United States might be dragged into 'another Vietnam'. The victorious MPLA established the People's Republic of Angola and concluded a treaty with the Soviet Union in 1976. The image of a virtual Soviet 'satellite' was conveyed by the continued presence of several thousand Cuban troops who remained in Angola ostensibly to protect the new republic from internal subversion and the threat of military incursions from South Africa.

A similar pattern of events occurred in East Africa, where the Soviets were particularly keen to support friendly radical governments and to acquire the use of naval bases to allow their navy easy access to the Indian Ocean. In 1974 the Soviets signed a treaty with Somalia that provided generous financial aid, military equipment and training for the Somali army. In response the United States sought to cultivate closer relations with Ethiopia, but this policy suffered a set-back in 1974 when Emperor Haile Selassie was overthrown and replaced by a Marxist military regime. The Soviets welcomed what they interpreted as a victory for 'national liberation' and a hindrance to American influence, but their satisfaction at the turn of events was tempered by the evident hostility between the new Ethiopian government and Somalia, arising from the latter's claim to sovereignty over the Ethiopian-controlled Ogaden territory. In July 1977 Somalia sent troops into Ethiopia to take possession of the Ogaden. In a 'reversal of alliances', the Soviets chose to support Ethiopia and, at that country's request, sent large quantities of military equipment including an airlift of up to 20,000 Cuban troops. As in Angola, the United States government was disturbed by the dispatch of Cuban forces beyond the western hemisphere, but was reluctant to aid Somalia because that country was clearly identified as the 'aggressor' in the conflict. The subsequent military victory of Ethiopia over Somalia was widely interpreted as a diplomatic victory for the Soviet Union.

The occurrence of Soviet intervention in Africa coincided with the overrunning of South Vietnam in 1975 by North Vietnam and shortly afterwards the establishment of communist governments in Cambodia (Kampuchea) and Laos. The result in the United States was a sense of humiliation that found itself reflected in the growing controversy over *détente*. Indeed, during the presidential election campaign in 1976 President Ford even instructed officials in his administration not to use the word '*détente*'. It was so controversial that it had to be replaced with 'peace through strength' (Garthoff, 1994a, p. 604). As Kissinger had remarked, however, it had never been envisaged that *détente* would end superpower competition in the Third World. The example of the Soviets seeking to exploit local conditions in Africa to their advantage was parallelled by the United States attempting to do the same in the Middle East. Moreover, the United States was hardly powerless and could also act unilaterally in its own sphere of influence, as had been demonstrated by the policy of 'destabilizing' the Marxist regime of Salvador Allende in Chile until that government was overthrown by an internal military coup in 1973. The weakness of *détente* was not so much the machinations of Soviet adventurism as the collapse of political support for Nixon and Kissinger within the United States. In part, this was because Nixon had raised too high the public expectations that would result from the 'era of negotiations'. Moreover, Americans were reluctant to accept the concept of 'parity' and could not give up the belief, nurtured since the late 1940s, that the Soviet Union was an adversarial power bent upon acquiring superiority over the United States in nuclear weapons and exploiting international crises in order to promote international communism. This attitude was reflected in the charges of American politicians that the Soviets could not be trusted to abide by the terms of SALT I or Basket III of the Helsinki Accords. In addition, the resulting political backlash within Congress against *détente* prevented Kissinger from employing 'linkage' to restrain Soviet behaviour in Sub-Saharan Africa. Indeed, Congress adopted its own form of 'linkage' and insisted on further complicating relations with the Soviet Union by denying that country most-favoured-nation (MFN) treatment and passing the Jackson–Vanik Amendment in 1974, which stated that American economic concessions must be contingent upon the Soviet government relaxing its restrictions on Jewish emigration from the Soviet Union. Nevertheless, Nixon and Kissinger had shown that *détente* could reduce tensions by promoting a constructive attitude towards negotiations and, in cases where the superpowers possessed mutual interests, lead to agreements that contributed to the maintenance of world peace and stability.

The End of *Détente*

The dissatisfaction of the American public with *détente* partly explained the victory of Jimmy Carter over Gerald Ford in the 1976 presidential election. In keeping with his image as a Washington 'outsider', the new president promised radical changes, including an end to the obsession with Cold War politics which he believed had for too long dominated American foreign policy and had resulted in the traumatic experience of the Vietnam War. Much more important in his opinion was the promotion of a cooperative global community in which emphasis would be placed on 'North–South' dialogue rather than East–West rivalry. Superpower relations were therefore to be subsumed within broader global issues such as the international economy, the problems of the Third World, and especially 'human rights'. I want our country to be the focal point for deep concern about human beings all over the world', stated Carter early in his administration (Brzezinski, 1983, p. 125). While Carter intended to condemn all governments that violated human rights, he was aware that the Soviet Union would incur the brunt of such criticism. 'I had made it clear in the campaign that I was not going to ignore Soviet abuse of human rights', he recalled (Carter, 1995, p. 150). Consequently, the United States government duly released statements of support for the activities of the monitoring groups set up by the Helsinki Accords. The Nobel Peace Prize winner from the Soviet Union, Andrei Sakharov, attracted particular attention and international publicity. Carter described Sakharov as 'the distinguished scientist and dissident'. To Brezhnev, he was 'a renegade who proclaimed himself an enemy of the Soviet state' (Carter, 1995, pp. 150–1. The Soviet leader warned the American government not to interfere in Soviet internal affairs.

As the question of human rights demonstrated, Carter soon found himself much more closely involved in East–West than in North–South relations. A similar imperative was exerted by the issue of arms control. In his inaugural address in January 1977 Carter had envisaged a future world in which all nuclear weapons would be eliminated. He also acknowledged that 'our best hope' in making significant progress towards achieving this aim lay not in North–South discussions but in concluding a SALT treaty with the Soviet Union (Carter, 1995, p. 218). Indeed, there was a general expectation at the beginning of the Carter administration that the SALT II agreement made by Ford and Brezhnev at Vladivostok in 1974 was virtually complete and was ready to be signed by the new president and the Soviet leader. But American politics intervened once again to upset the SALT process. As a Democratic president, Carter did not want to be too closely identified with an agreement negotiated by the previous Republican administration. Consequently, he unveiled his own alternative proposal, containing 'deep cuts' that would reduce the total of missiles to one-third of the figure provisionally agreed in 1974 for land-based ICBMs. Since the latter weapons were the main element of the Soviet nuclear forces, the Soviets suspected that the Americans were seeking to upset the nuclear balance. In rejecting Carter's proposals, the Soviet foreign minister, Andrei Gromyko, dismissed them as a 'cheap and shady manoeuvre' intended to secure 'unilateral advantages' for the United States (Talbott, 1979, p. 74).

The result was an impasse in negotiations that would not be broken until 1979. During this period both sides continued to modernize their respective nuclear arsenals. The Soviet Union developed new MIRVed offensive missiles, notably the SS-20, and began deployment of the Backfire supersonic bomber in 1977. The United States unveiled several new weapons systems, including the Missile Experimental (MX) MIRVed missile, ground-launched cruise missiles (GLCMs), and the Enhanced Radiation Weapon (ERW) or 'neutron' bomb, which was designed to spread radiation to kill soldiers but to cause limited damage to buildings and equipment. Despite the weapons build-up, however, both super-powers still wanted arms control. They showed this by continuing to observe the limits contained in SALT I even though the agreement had formally expired in 1977. In fact, Carter had no doubt that a new SALT treaty was in America's 'national interest'. Echoing the ideas of Nixon and Kissinger, he explained:

> To reject SALT II would mean that the inevitable competition in strategic nuclear arms would grow even more dangerous. Each crisis, each confrontation, each point of friction – as serious as it may be in its own right – would take on an added measure of significance and an added dimension of danger. It is precisely because we have fundamental differences with the Soviet Union that we are determined to bring this dangerous dimension of our military competition under control. (Carter, 1995, p. 243)

The SALT II treaty was eventually signed by Carter and Brezhnev at the Vienna summit in June 1979. The agreement was intended to last until 1985 and limited each side to 2,250 strategic nuclear delivery vehicles of which no more than 1,320 could be MIRVed missiles. Although the acceptance of numerical equality by the Soviets implied a gain for the United States, the high overall total of missiles allowed in the final agreement represented a rejection of Carter's original proposal of 'deep cuts'. Moreover, like the 1972 treaty, SALT II was a compromise that deliberately omitted particular weapons and placed minimal restrictions on future research and development. For example, the Soviet Backfire was not included because it was defined as a 'medium range' rather than a 'long-range' bomber. Similarly, the United States could proceed with the development of the Trident submarine, the cruise missile and the MX. Ironically, however, the large number of MIRVed missiles allowed and the lack of restrictions on future weapons developments stimulated opposition to the treaty in the United States. A prominent critic was the diplomat Paul Nitze, who reiterated Reagan's charge that the treaty was too advantageous to the Soviets. 'It is time for the United States to stand up and not be a patsy', Nitze told the United States Senate (Paterson et al., 1995, p. 903). Carter attempted to mollify opponents of the treaty by announcing a substantial increase in American defence spending. Responding to the reported emplacement of Soviet MIRVed SS-20s targeted on Western Europe, he also revealed plans to strengthen NATO by deploying several hundred medium-range Pershing II missiles and cruise missiles in Western Europe. Nevertheless, the debate to ratify SALT II continued its uncertain course until January 1980, when President Carter dramatically withdrew the treaty from the Senate as a mark of American protest against the Soviet invasion of Afghanistan.

The difficulties experienced in negotiating and attempting to ratify SALT II indicated the faltering of *détente* during the late 1970s. Another example of the growing discord between the superpowers was the Carter administration's calculated resort to playing the 'China card' in order to put diplomatic pressure on the Soviets. Since Nixon's dramatic visit to Beijing in 1972 relations between the United States and China had been allowed to stagnate. After the death of Mao Zedong in 1976, however, the new Chinese leadership under Deng Xiaoping chose to develop closer economic and political relations with the West and especially the United States. Like Nixon in 1971, President Carter responded positively. Describing the establishment of full diplomatic relations with China as 'a key strategic goal', Carter's national security adviser, Zbigniew Brzezinski, remarked: 'We were convinced that a genuinely cooperative relationship between Washington and Beijing would greatly enhance the stability of the Far East and that, more generally, it would be to U.S. advantage in the global competition with the Soviet Union' (Brzezinski, 1983, p. 196). In contrast to Kissinger's 'triangular diplomacy', the United States no longer sought to act in a balancing role but intended to side with China to gain geopolitical advantage over the Soviet Union. Full diplomatic relations between the United States and the People's Republic of China were established in January 1979. When he reported news of this development to the Soviet ambassador, Anatoly Dobrynin, Brzezinski gleefully noted that the Soviet diplomat 'looked absolutely stunned' (Brzezinski, 1983, p. 232).

Although the Soviets were dismayed by the *rapprochement* between the United States and China and the impasse over SALT II, the most acute divergence in superpower relations arose directly from events in Iran and Afghanistan. These countries were in the central part of the region that stretched from the Horn of Africa to Pakistan and was dubbed 'the arc of crisis' by Brzezinski. The term was novel, but the reference to 'crisis' was hardly new. Preserving Western access to the oil-rich Middle East had been a long-standing feature of American diplomacy and was given heightened importance by the Arab–Israeli conflict, the withdrawal of British military influence 'east of Suez', the activities of OPEC and the resulting 'oil shocks'. During the 1970s the United States directed considerable effort to cultivating a special relationship with Iran and its ruler, Shah Mohammed Reza Pahlevi. The policy was highly successful. 'Alone among the countries of the region – Israel aside – Iran made friendship with the United States the starting point of its foreign policy', noted Kissinger (Kissinger, 1979, p. 1262). But Iranian society was riven with internal tensions. Muslim fundamentalists denounced the autocratic rule of the shah and blamed American influence for his attempts to impose alien, 'Western' reforms. A prominent religious leader, the Ayatollah Khomeini, castigated the United States as 'the great Satan'. Consequently, the overthrow of the shah in 1979 followed by the establishment of an Islamic republic ruled by Khomeini was a major blow for American policy. Moreover, although the Iranian revolution was not inspired by communism, its overtly anti-American and anti-Western character posed a threat to Western influence throughout the Middle East. This was exemplified in November 1979 when Iranian students occupied the American embassy in Tehran and held 69 Americans hostage. Despite an abortive American attempt to free the hostages in 1980, they remained captive until January 1981. The damaging effects of the prolonged 'hostage crisis' upon American prestige were considerable and some critics charged that presidential weakness had 'lost' Iran just as it had 'lost' China in 1949. 'Iran was the Carter Administration's greatest setback', summed up Brzezinski (Brzezinski, 1983, p. 354).

While American diplomats observed the collapse of a decade of their efforts to build up Iran as an ally of the West, the Soviet Union invaded Iran's northern neighbour, Afghanistan, in December 1979. Like the Russian empire during the nineteenth century, the Soviet Union had maintained a close interest in the affairs of Afghanistan, a country with which it shared a 1,500-mile border. Intervention in 1979 was prompted by the fear that the pro-Soviet government in Afghanistan was likely to fall from power and that this would be severely detrimental to the national interest of the Soviet Union. The invasion initially involved up to 80,000 troops and was notably the first overt use of the Red Army since 1945 outside the areas occupied during World War II. No doubt the Soviet military hoped for a repeat of the successful operations mounted in Hungary in 1956 and Czechoslovakia in 1968, but subsequent events demonstrated that they had seriously underestimated the degree of fanatical nationalist resistance that the invasion would arouse. The military incursion into Afghanistan soon began to resemble the 'Vietnam quagmire' as Soviet troops exceeded 100,000 and the financial and human cost of the war steadily increased.

In January 1980 the United Nations condemned the blatant aggression of the Soviet Union against Afghanistan. The Soviets, however, used their veto in the Security Council to prevent any repetition of the military retaliation that the UN had taken against North Korea for invading South Korea in 1950. They might also have calculated that the Carter administration would respond passively as it had done over the Ogaden War and the fall of the shah. But President Carter was personally surprised and shocked by the invasion. 'This action of the Soviets', he revealed, 'has made a more dramatic change in my own opinion of what the Soviet's ultimate goals are than anything they've done in the previous time I've been in office' (Garthoff, 1994a, pp. 1059–60). Drawing parallels not only with the expansionist ambitions ascribed to Stalin after 1945 but with Hitler during the 1930s, American officials pondered over whether the invasion was the first stage in Brezhnev's strategic master plan to control the Persian Gulf. Carter explained: 'If the Soviets could consolidate their hold on Afghanistan, the balance of power in the entire region would be drastically modified in their favor, and they might be tempted toward further aggression. We were resolved to do everything feasible to prevent such a turn of events' (Carter, 1995, pp. 482–3).

Although the Carter administration never publicly announced the abandonment of *détente*, the measures taken against the Soviet Union in 1980 signified a definite reversal of American policy. For example, the decision to withdraw the SALT II treaty from the Senate effectively halted progress on the issue of arms control, which had provided the catalyst for *détente* a decade earlier. Similarly, the imposition of an embargo on American agricultural exports to the Soviet Union was a deliberate blow against the concept of mutually beneficial economic cooperation. Moreover, Carter's call for an international boycott of the Olympic Games scheduled to be held in Moscow in July 1980 reflected a determination to be awkward and uncooperative. More ominously the United States revived the policy of military containment. In his State of the Union Address of January 1980 Carter declared: 'Let our position be absolutely clear: An attempt by any outside force to gain control of the Persian Gulf region will be regarded as an assault on the vital interests of the United States of America, and such an assault will be repelled by use of any means necessary, including military force' (Carter, 1995, p. 492). The warning was not empty rhetoric. An American deterrent to aggression was to be provided by the creation of a 100,000-strong Rapid Deployment Force (RDF), which would be locally based and whose purpose would be to respond quickly to crises within the region.

The Carter administration had initially intended to concentrate on North–South developmental issues and international cooperation. Instead, it found that its foreign policy was dominated by Cold War politics. President Carter was genuinely dismayed at Soviet aggression against 'a freedom-loving people' (Carter, 1995, p. 481), but he also understood the need to display American strength and decisiveness to counteract the impression of weakness and drift associated with the humiliating and still unresolved Iranian 'hostage crisis'. There was also criticism that the president's preoccupation with human rights had facilitated the rise of communist movements in Latin America, especially in Nicaragua and El Salvador. Moreover, political circumstances indicated that a tough stance against the Soviet Union was likely to win votes in the 1980 presidential election. This proved correct, but the result was a victory for the even 'tougher' Republican candidate, Ronald Reagan.

Analogies were drawn between the 'Carter Doctrine' and the earlier 'Truman Doctrine', but there was a difference in that Carter did not receive the same degree of support from the Western alliance which Truman had enjoyed in 1947. Although they recognized the importance of maintaining political stability in the oil-rich Persian Gulf, the Western European powers did not want 'out-of-area' considerations to damage the profitable economic contacts that they had built up with the Soviet Union and Eastern Europe during the 1970s. 'We will not permit ten years of *détente* and defense policy to be destroyed', declared the West German chancellor, Helmut Schmidt (Dunbabin, 1994, p. 331). Nevertheless, the pursuit of *détente*, as originally formulated by Nixon and Kissinger, could not be sustained and was ended in 1980 when Carter deliberately used the language of confrontation to raise rather than reduce tensions between the superpowers. *Détente* had been successful in facilitating and stimulating cooperation between the United States and the Soviet Union, most notably in arms control and European security. However, disagreement over crises in the Third World highlighted the fundamental limitations of *détente* and ushered in what some commentators described as the 'Second Cold War'.

6

End of the Cold War

Reagan Confronts the Evil Empire

During the first half of the 1980s Ronald Reagan was the dominant figure in Cold War politics. Although he came to office in 1981 with minimal experience of diplomacy, the new American president held strong views about his country's duty to act as the leader of the 'free world.' Most of all he was deeply distrustful of communism, and a tone of strident anti-communism reminiscent of John Foster Dulles and the 1950s was evident in a number of speeches delivered during the first term of his presidency. Especially notorious and provocative was the description in 1983 of the Soviet Union as 'an evil empire' and the 'focus of evil in the world' (Oberdorfer, 1992, p. 22). Reagan also complained that diplomatic negotiations with the Soviets were inherently difficult and frustrating because 'the only morality they recognize is what will further their cause, meaning they reserve unto themselves the right to commit any crime to lie, to cheat' (Haig, 1984, pp. 102–30). This explained the failure of *détente*, which the unscrupulous Soviets had turned into a 'one-way street' to their own selfish advantage. Consequently, Reagan rejected *détente* in favour of a policy of standing firm, building up American military power and resolving only 'to negotiate from a position of strength' (Reagan, 1990, p. 549). To the Soviet leadership, it was evident that the new administration clearly preferred confrontation to negotiation. The Politburo member, Konstantin Chernenko, observed that, 'the process of militarization in the West has entered a new, much more dangerous phase' (Garthoff, 1994b, p. 62).

Reagan's aggressive and confrontational approach to super-power relations produced an old-fashioned 'war of words' in which American officials constantly asserted the superiority of democracy over the totalitarian values of the Soviet Union. In a speech to the British Parliament in March 1982, Reagan stressed America's historic sense of mission to promote the cause of human liberty throughout the world: 'Freedom is not the sole prerogative of a lucky few, but the inalienable and universal right of all human beings' (Melanson, 1991, p. 141). The president's positive assertion of the universality of Western values became popularly known as the 'Reagan Doctrine' and was calculated to pose a direct challenge to the contention of the Brezhnev Doctrine that the establishment of a communist state could not be reversed. Exploiting the adverse international publicity suffered by the Soviets as a result of their invasion of Afghanistan and the growing perception that Moscow had become a force for imperialism rather than liberation, Reagan publicly praised the activities of 'freedom fighters' who were seeking to overturn pro-Soviet regimes in the Third World. 'We must not break faith with those who are risking their lives – on every continent, from Afghanistan to Nicaragua – to defy Soviet-supported aggression and secure rights which have been ours from birth', he affirmed (Melanson, 1991, p. 159).

Although he ruled out direct American military intervention, Reagan backed up his words of support for 'freedom fighters' with substantial material aid, usually given secretly by the CIA in the form of money and military equipment. In Afghanistan, weapons including the highly effective anti-aircraft Stinger missile were dispatched to the rebels from across the Afghan border with Pakistan. CIA activities on a smaller scale were conducted in Angola, Ethiopia and Kampuchea (Cambodia). Much more public and controversial, however, was the policy pursued in Central America, where Reagan sought to rectify what he regarded as a major error of the Carter administration in tacitly approving the overthrow in 1979 of 'friendly' authoritarian rulers in El Salvador and Nicaragua. The result had been an intensification of communist insurgency in El Salvador and the establishment of a Marxist government in Nicaragua. The Nicaraguan government was formed by representatives of the Sandinista National Liberation Front (FSLN) and was more popularly referred to as the 'Sandinistas', a name derived from César Augusto Sandino a celebrated Nicaraguan nationalist and anti-American hero of the 1920s and 1930s.

Officials in the Reagan administration observed events in Central America primarily in terms of Cold War politics. They were alarmed by the spread of Cuban and Soviet influence in El Salvador and Nicaragua and feared the application of a domino effect in which communism, if unchecked, would expand irresistibly throughout the region. 'The situation in Central America', remarked Secretary of State George Shultz 'was a problem of immense importance to the United States, and I knew we had to confront it' (Shultz, 1993, p. 285). The result was substantial American financial and military assistance for the 'democratic' government of El Salvador to suppress the pro-communist rebels. In the process, the rebels were denied military victory, but El Salvador came to resemble war-torn South Vietnam during the early 1960s. A quite different policy was pursued in Nicaragua because the American objective was not to maintain but to overthrow that country's government. The Sandinistas were to be 'destabilized' by applying a combination of external economic pressure and internal civil disorder. The CIA organized and financed an army of guerrillas known as the 'Contras' (abbreviation of 'counter-revolutionaries') who operated from bases in neighbouring Honduras and Costa Rica. While Reagan referred to the Contras as 'freedom fighters', the Sandinistas denounced them as traitors and mercenaries in the pay of the United States. Influenced by the 'Vietnam syndrome', American political opinion was sharply divided over the issue of Central America. The fear of being sucked into 'another Vietnam' not only ruled out the use of American combat troops but also seriously restricted the amount of financial support that Congress would vote to assist the Contras. This prompted the Reagan administration to resort to covert methods of funding the Contras, including the diversion of money gained from secret arms sales to Iran. The illegal action was publicly revealed in 1986 and resulted in the Iran–Contra scandal. The withdrawal of American material support compelled the Contras to agree to a cease-fire in 1988. The Sandinistas, therefore, remained in government through the years of Reagan's presidency. They eventually lost power after being defeated in national elections held in 1990.

Any suggestion of American weakness in retaining control of its 'backyard' was rebutted by the decisive action of the Reagan administration in dispatching American troops to intervene in the

Caribbean island of Grenada in October 1983. This was the first overt instance of direct American military intervention in Latin America since 1965, when Johnson had ordered an invasion of the Dominican Republic. Like Johnson, Reagan argued that intervention was necessary to defeat the forces of communism, who were attempting to establish 'a Soviet-Cuban colony' that would be used 'as a major military base to export terror and undermine democracy' (Melanson, 1991, pp. 170–1). The Reagan administration also insisted that the operation was not an 'invasion' but a 'rescue mission' designed to stop an unfriendly government from carrying out a plan to provoke a potential hostage crisis by seizing a group of American medical students resident on the island. The exact reason for the intervention remained uncertain, but critics were effectively disarmed by its rapid success. Secretary of State Shultz jubilantly noted that the firm action of the United States in Grenada demonstrated that 'some Western democracies were again ready to use the military strength they had harbored and built up over the years in defense of their principles and interests' (Shultz, 1993, p. 340).

The promise to restore America's international prestige and seek only to negotiate with the Soviet Union from a position of strength had been a prominent feature of Reagan's successful presidential campaign in 1980. This would be achieved by rebuilding American military power and thereby reversing what was perceived in the United States as a decade of neglect, during which the Soviets had been allowed to gain a lead in strategic weapons. In order to close 'the window of [American] vulnerability' as fast as possible and replace it with a 'margin of safety', defence spending was more than doubled from 1981 to 1986. The result was the largest American arms build-up since the scare over the 'missile gap' in the early 1960s, and almost equal to that undertaken at the time of NSC-68 and the Korean War during the 1950s. In fact, the scale of rearmament was so substantial that the Reagan administration appeared to be seeking not parity with but nuclear superiority over the Soviets. This was underlined by the emphasis placed on restoring high-profile programmes that had been cancelled by the Carter administration, namely the MX missile and the B-1 bomber. Also included was the Advanced Technology Bomber (ATB) or Stealth bomber, equipped with technology to make the plane invisible to radar.

The most ambitious, expensive and controversial new weapons system was, however, the Strategic Defense Initiative (SDI). As Reagan explained in first announcing the programme in March 1983, the purpose of SDI was to set up weapons in outer space which would provide a protective shield to defend the United States from missile attack. Although this seemed to mark a major escalation of the arms race, Reagan argued that SDI would achieve the very opposite because its implementation would provide absolute security against offensive nuclear missiles and consequently make those weapons redundant. The president painted a picture of a future world at peace: 'What if free people could live secure in the knowledge that their security did not rest upon the threat of instant U.S. retaliation to deter a Soviet attack, that we could intercept and destroy strategic ballistic missiles before they reached our own soil or that of our allies?' (Shultz, 1993, p. 257). In theory, the nightmare of 'mutual assured destruction' would be replaced by the much more comfortable scenario of 'mutual assured survival'. In 1983, however, SDI was very much at a preliminary experimental stage. Indeed, the idea of 'Star Wars', in which battle stations located in outer space exchanged laser beams with each other, attracted considerable incredulity and ridicule. Nevertheless, the concept reflected the same American faith and prowess in science and applied technology that had produced the atomic bomb in 1945 and had been followed by a stream of new weapons. It was therefore treated very seriously by the Soviets and became a highly contentious issue in ensuing arms talks between the superpowers. The new Soviet leader, Yury Andropov, queried whether SDI infringed the 1972 ABM treaty and warned that the United States was embarking upon 'an extremely dangerous path' (Shultz, 1993, p. 260).

Although alarmist rumours frequently circulated in the American press that the Reagan administration was intending to achieve sufficient military power to win a nuclear war against the Soviets, there is no evidence that Reagan wanted war. Indeed, within one year of becoming president he surprised both his allies and adversaries by agreeing to observe the limits on strategic weapons contained in the unratified SALT II treaty and to enter into talks with the Soviets on European security. The negotiations, which opened at Geneva in November 1981, concerned the disposition in Europe of missiles with an 'intermediate' range of up to 3,000 miles and known technically as intermediate-range nuclear forces (INFs).

The weapons directly involved were the Soviet SS-20s, several hundred of which were already in position, and American cruise and Pershing II missiles, whose deployment in Western Europe was projected to take place in 1983. At the beginning of the Geneva conference the American delegates confounded the Soviets by proposing the 'zero option', in which American cancellation of the future deployment of cruise and Pershing II missiles would be matched by the dismantling of Soviet INFs. In effect, the United States was offering to maintain its INFs at zero if the Soviets reduced their number of INFs to zero. Much as he had done in response to Carter's 'deep cuts' in 1977, Soviet Foreign Minister Gromyko vehemently rejected the proposal as 'unilateral disarmament' (Shultz, 1993, p. 123). In fact, it was hardly to the strategic advantage of the Soviets to remove 'real' missiles in exchange for an American undertaking not to deploy 'notional' missiles. Moreover, the arms build-up instituted by Reagan had alarmed European opinion and provoked public demonstrations in Western Europe in favour of world peace and a 'freeze' on all nuclear weapons. The diplomatic pressure on the Reagan administration was further increased by 'Moscow's propaganda machinery [which] unleashed a major campaign in every European country' (Kissinger, 1994, p. 777). It was very likely, therefore, that the controversial deployment of American INFs would be cancelled for political reasons.

The zero option was so unpalatable to the Soviets and its rejection by them so predictable that it was widely regarded at the time as a tactical ploy by the Americans to sabotage the deliberations of the Geneva conference while gaining credit for having advocated a measure of significant disarmament. A similar ulterior motive was attributed to Reagan's proposal in May 1982 to resume strategic arms talks under the title of Strategic Arms Reduction Talks (START). The new description reflected Reagan's understandable desire to dissociate himself from the SALT process which he had denounced so virulently throughout the 1970s. However, the replacement of the word 'limitations' by 'reductions' aroused controversy, because the Soviets interpreted it as a blatant attempt by the Americans to gain a strategic advantage. The Soviet nuclear strike force contained a higher proportion of land-based ICBMs than the much more mobile American triad. Consequently, as with Carter's proposed 'deep cuts' in 1977, a substantial reduction of existing strategic weapons, without any distinction being made of particular type of weapon, would be strategically disadvantageous to the Soviets because they would have to give up more ICBMs than the Americans. Although the START talks commenced on schedule in Geneva in June 1982, they made little progress and were suspended in December 1983. Soviet Foreign Minister Gromyko blamed the United States. 'Rather than pursue negotiations and display a desire to seek agreements,' he argued, 'the U.S. administration has set out to upset the existing correlation of [military] forces' (Oberdorfer, 1992, p. 73).

The negative attitude shown by Gromyko in the arms talks reflected Soviet resistance to Reagan's professed determination 'to negotiate from a position of strength'. There was also calculation that a waiting game was sensible so long as the United States and its Western European allies appeared to be deeply divided over the question of INFs in Europe. However, the deployment of American INFs in Western Europe on schedule in 1983 not only boosted the nuclear retaliatory power of the West but also upset Soviet hopes of a serious split emerging between the Western allies. 'The Soviets had suffered a severe propaganda defeat', gloated Secretary of State Shultz, and he added: 'With deployments under way, our position was one of strength' (Shultz, 1993, p. 377). According to Western intelligence reports there was evidence that the Soviets even feared that the American INFs were meant to be used in a first-strike nuclear attack on the Soviet Union in November 1983. Relations were particularly tense as a result of American anger at the shooting down on 31 August of Korean Air Lines Flight 007, a South Korean civilian plane that had strayed into Soviet airspace over Siberia. Indeed, the Soviets appeared to have been unprepared for the collapse of *détente* and Reagan's vigorous assertion of American leadership of the West. By contrast, Soviet diplomacy seemed to be drifting into a state of paralysis. One major reason was the lack of effective leadership caused by the death of Brezhnev in November 1982 and the fact that the next two general secretaries, Yury Andropov and Konstantin Chernenko, were both in ill health and held office for a relatively short period. The end of the rule of the 'gerontocracy' was signified by the death of Chernenko in March 1985 and the rise to power of Mikhail Gorbachev.

Gorbachev in Power

Appointed general secretary at the relatively young age of 54, Gorbachev displayed a confident and energetic public persona that would dominate the international spotlight for the rest of the decade. The implications for superpower relations were immediately apparent. After his first meeting with the new general secretary, Shultz reported: 'In Gorbachev we have an entirely different kind of leader in the Soviet Union than we have experienced before' (Shultz, 1993, p. 532). The sudden emergence of a younger generation of Soviet political figures was further confirmed in May 1985 when Gorbachev appointed Eduard Shevardnadze as foreign minister in place of Andrei Gromyko, who had held the office continuously since 1957 and had become a virtual personification of the Cold War. Shultz noted that Shevardnadze could 'smile, engage, converse' and presented a 'breathtaking' contrast to Gromyko (Shultz, 1993, p. 702).

Dismissing the Brezhnev era as 'years of stagnation', Gorbachev boldly announced his intention of taking radical initiatives to transform the Soviet Union both politically and economically. Emphasis was placed on bringing 'openness' (*glasnost*) into the political system, while 'restructuring' (*perestroika*) was introduced into the economy. Gorbachev also recognized that the success of his internal reforms depended upon a reversal of the long-standing policy of allocating a disproportionate share of the Soviet gross national product to military purposes. In this context it was vitally important to reduce the risk of war by improving relations with the West and especially the United States. Gorbachev was keen to travel and meet personally with Western leaders. Most of all, he sought to impress upon them that the Soviet Union wished to be a partner and not an adversary. In marked contrast to the usual rhetoric of Cold War politics, he called for 'new thinking' in international relations to reduce political tensions and military competition. Before becoming general secretary Gorbachev had visited London in December 1984 and had persuaded the British prime minister, Margaret Thatcher, that he was a man with whom the West could do business. President Reagan had shown no great desire to meet personally with Gorbachev's three predecessors, but he was receptive to the new leader's overtures and readily agreed to a summit meeting. Despite his 'cold warrior' rhetoric, Reagan was genuinely in favour of an agreement that would lead to substantial reductions in nuclear weapons. Indeed, his tough anti-communist image was useful in deflecting domestic criticism that, by meeting with Gorbachev, he was engaging in *détente* or that he might be seeking to appease the Soviets. Moreover, like Gorbachev, the president was also a pragmatic politician who was aware of the need to reduce the huge deficits in the American budget arising from his policy of increasing military spending and, at the same time, lowering federal taxes.

The meeting of Reagan and Gorbachev took place at Geneva in November 1985. It represented the first summit of superpower leaders since Carter and Brezhnev had met in Vienna in 1979. On this occasion, however, there was no important treaty to sign. In fact, the Geneva summit was regarded as a public relations exercise whose purpose was for both leaders to appear as world statesmen while providing an opportunity for each man to learn more about the other. In this sense, the summit was a success because both men established an immediate personal rapport. As Roosevelt had claimed after his first meeting with Stalin, Reagan would later remark in similar vein that he 'liked' his Soviet counterpart and that 'there was a chemistry between Gorbachev and me that produced something very close to friendship' (Reagan, 1990, p. 707). The president also favourably impressed the Soviet leader. 'I realized by the end of our two-day meeting that Ronald Reagan too was a man "you could do business with"', noted Gorbachev (Gorbachev, 1996, p. 405). In the actual substantive discussions between the two leaders, the question of strategic arms reductions received the most prominence. Gorbachev was particularly critical of SDI, which he described as 'offensive nuclear weapons circling the earth'. Reagan insisted, however, that the programme was 'purely defensive'. A joint communiqué was issued in which both governments agreed to 'accelerate the work' on arms control, so that there might be 'early progress' in holding discussions to prevent an arms race in space and implement substantial cuts amounting to a 50 per cent reduction in strategic offensive weapons (Talbott, 1989, pp. 285–6, 289).

Seeking to create a momentum to follow on from the Geneva summit, Gorbachev made a public announcement in January 1986 calling for the elimination of all nuclear weapons by the end of the century. It was now, however, the turn of the Americans to respond negatively to what they described as a Soviet 'peace offensive' designed mainly to attract the attention of the international media. American officials believed that the proposal was intentionally so wide-ranging that it would include the suspension of all research into SDI. Writing to Reagan in September, Gorbachev lamented that there had been 'no movement' in the arms talks. 'They will lead nowhere unless you and I intervene personally', he concluded (Oberdorfer, 1992, p. 186). The result was a hastily arranged meeting between the two leaders at Reykjavik in October 1986. The remote Icelandic capital was chosen because it was roughly half-way between Washington and Moscow. The Americans assumed that the president was attending a 'preliminary meeting' rather than a 'summit' and anticipated that the discussions would concentrate on preparations for a full-scale summit scheduled to take place in Washington during 1987. Gorbachev, however, saw Reykjavik as a unique opportunity to engage in face-to-face diplomacy and persuade Reagan to accept a major breakthrough in arms reductions. It seemed that his efforts would be crowned with astounding success when the two leaders approved an ambitious variant of the zero option that would halve their offensive strategic missiles over the next five years and dismantle all nuclear missiles within ten years. At one point they even appeared to consent to the elimination of *all* nuclear weapons. Once again, however, SDI prevented the conclusion of a remarkable agreement. 'I have promised the American people I will not give up SDI', Reagan told Gorbachev. The Soviet leader curtly replied that the halting of SDI was 'everything' (Oberdorfer, 1992, p. 203).

The Reykjavik meeting ended in failure. The disappointment was more keenly felt because the attendant media had been informed that a historic agreement on arms control was imminent. Nevertheless, senior military and political figures in the West privately expressed relief at the inconclusive outcome. They had not been directly consulted during the talks and were wary of crucially important decisions being made over which they exercised minimal control. For example, the governments of Britain and France were particularly concerned about the implications for the future of their own independent nuclear forces. There was also suspicion that, by removing their missiles from Europe, the Americans were falling into a Soviet trap designed to separate or 'decouple' the United States from its European allies. Moreover, a 'denuclearized' Europe might please advocates of disarmament, but it would place the West at a serious military disadvantage so long as the Soviets possessed overwhelming superiority in conventional forces.

Despite the contemporary perception that the Reykjavik meeting had been a 'near disaster or near farce', Secretary of State Shultz believed that its 'achievements' were 'greater than those in any U.S.–Soviet meeting before' (Shultz, 1993, p. 776). Shultz based his optimism upon the fact that the Soviets had essentially accepted the zero option. This was confirmed in February 1987 when Gorbachev indicated that he was willing to negotiate an agreement specifically covering INFs in Europe. Significantly, SDI was not mentioned. Whether this was the consequence of Reagan's firmness at Geneva and Reykjavik or Gorbachev's statesmanlike vision is debatable. The fact was that the Soviets finally recognized that SDI was non-negotiable and that to insist on its inclusion simply prevented agreement on other substantive issues. After some months of complex negotiations the Intermediate-Range and Shorter-Range Missiles Treaty (INF Treaty) was made ready for signature by Reagan and Gorbachev at the Washington summit in December 1987. By eliminating all American and Soviet INFs – including SS-20s, Pershing IIs and cruise missiles – from Europe within three years, the treaty effectively implemented the 'zero option' originally proposed by the United States in 1981. In fact, the actual arrangement was described as 'global double zero' because the Soviets agreed to eliminate not only their INFs located in Europe but also those in the Far East. In return, the Americans would dismantle their INFs in North America. Partly to vindicate the president's strategy of negotiating from strength, the Reagan administration conveyed the impression to the American press that the Soviet Union had made more concessions than the United States. This was reinforced by the statistics contained within the treaty, which showed that the Soviets would destroy 1,846 weapons while the corresponding figure for the United States was 846. In addition, Gorbachev accepted arrangements for Western inspection and verification of the dismantling process and agreed also to the exclusion of British and French missiles from the provisions of the treaty.

The INF treaty was the first strategic arms agreement to be negotiated between the superpowers for almost a decade. In contrast to SALT I and II, the 1987 treaty not only achieved 'reductions' rather than 'limitations', but actually eliminated an entire category of nuclear missiles. 'We had reached a new level of trust in our relations with the United States and initiated a genuine disarmament process', proudly remarked Gorbachev (Gorbachev, 1996, p. 445). Though it was not without critics in the United States, the treaty was successfully ratified by the American Senate in May 1988. The vote was taken just in time for Reagan and Gorbachev to exchange formal instruments of ratification during their summit meeting in Moscow. The summit marked a major public relations success for Gorbachev and highlighted the vast improvement in relations between the superpowers since his accession to power. The Soviet leader was especially gratified to welcome the first American president to visit Moscow since Nixon in 1974. Only a few years earlier Reagan had castigated the Soviet Union as an 'evil empire'. When questioned in Moscow whether the statement still applied, he replied much to Gorbachev's delight: 'No. I was talking about another time, another era' (Garthoff, 1994b, p. 352). The American president was even willing to deliver a speech in front of a giant bust of Lenin at Moscow State University. Reagan described his visit as 'a grand historical moment' (Oberdorfer, 1992, p. 295). To Gorbachev it represented 'another milestone marking the end of the Cold War' (Gorbachev, 1996, p. 450).

The impetus for further disarmament was boosted by a series of initiatives taken by Gorbachev to effect a significant Soviet military disengagement from Eastern Europe and the Third World. In November 1988 the Soviet leader appeared at the United Nations and announced a substantial unilateral cut in Soviet military forces, amounting to 500,000 men and 10,000 tanks. The reductions would be made mostly from troops currently stationed in Eastern Europe. Cuts in the number of conventional forces in Europe also resulted from the reopening of the MBFR talks in 1989 under the new name of the Conventional Armed Forces in Europe (CFE) talks. Beyond Europe, Gorbachev sought to liquidate what he believed to have been unwise and costly overseas commitments undertaken by Brezhnev. The most significant was the decision to end the war in Afghanistan, a struggle that had dragged on for almost a decade and had taken the lives of more than 30,000 Soviet troops. In early 1988 Gorbachev declared that all Soviet troops would be pulled out of Afghanistan within ten months. The operation was completed on schedule in February 1989. In Africa Soviet diplomatic pressure brought about a similar withdrawal of Cuban troops from Ethiopia and Angola. In addition, a substantial reduction in military and economic aid to Cuba was implemented in 1991. Whether these developments reflected a conscious desire to placate the United States is uncertain, but they undoubtedly indicated a distinct change in Soviet political and strategic priorities. Indeed, Gorbachev's dynamic and imaginative efforts to achieve world peace earned him admiration in the West resulting in the award of the Nobel Peace Prize in 1990, and the honour of being chosen as *Time* magazine's 'Man of the Year' for 1990. Scenes of 'Gorbymania' were a regular occurrence whenever the Soviet leader came to Western capitals.

The Collapse of Communism

In 1989–90 the Soviet empire of Eastern European satellite nations suddenly collapsed and was followed in 1991 by the disintegration of the Soviet Union itself. It appeared that the Soviets could also 'lose' a country and that the 'domino theory' did work after all, but in favour of the West rather than the East. In keeping with the historical theory that 'revolutions' are most often caused by rising rather than lower expectations, the rejection of communism in Eastern Europe was sparked by Gorbachev's reforming activities in the Soviet Union. His denunciation of the harm caused to the Soviet people by Brezhnev's 'years of stagnation' applied equally to political and economic conditions in the satellite states. Consequently, the introduction of *glasnost* and *perestroika* in the Soviet Union stimulated movements for the same fundamental reforms in Eastern Europe. In the process, the power and authority of local communist bosses were seriously challenged and swept away.

A similar pattern of events had occurred after Khrushchev's condemnation of Stalin's 'cult of personality' in 1956. Whereas Khrushchev had dispatched tanks to Hungary to crush signs of open armed rebellion, Gorbachev responded very differently. The countries of Eastern Europe were now regarded as economic liabilities rather than assets. Moreover, their military significance as defensive buffers was considerably diminished by the achievement of strategic arms reductions. In fact, contrary to some American fears, acceptance of the 'zero option' reflected Gorbachev's desire not to 'decouple' the United States from Western Europe but to facilitate the process of Soviet military disengagement from Eastern Europe, which he had unilaterally announced in his speech at the United Nations in December 1988. The popular risings against communist authority in Eastern Europe did not lead, therefore, to the dispatch of Soviet troops to enforce the Brezhnev Doctrine. Indeed, Gorbachev took a positive view of developments that promoted *perestroika* and did not appear to consider that they might result in the emergence of anti-communist and anti-Soviet governments. 'If we can bring people back into the socialist system instead of alienating them,' the Soviet leader optimistically remarked in July 1989, 'we can give socialism a second wind' (Stokes, 1993, p. 75). The purpose was not to stimulate separation or grant independence but to inspire much-needed reform and modernization. In retrospect, Gorbachev's miscalculation was that *perestroika* was not able to succeed either in the Soviet Union or in Eastern Europe.

Poland provided the first major challenge to communist political control. The focus of opposition to the government was the trade union movement 'Solidarity', led by the shipyard worker Lech Walesa. Solidarity had been formed in 1980, but was subsequently brutally repressed and denied legal status until April 1989. Candidates representing Solidarity enjoyed spectacular success in relatively free elections held in June. The result was the formation in August of a coalition government headed by Tadeusz Mazowiecki, who became the first non-communist prime minister in Eastern Europe for almost 40 years. No Soviet military retaliation was forthcoming. In effect, the Polish Communist Party had peacefully given up political power with the consent of the Soviet Union. Similar developments occurred in Hungary and Czechoslovakia, where the pace of political change was even more rapid. In Hungary Janos Kadar resigned in 1988 after more than 30 years in power, and elections in March 1990 gave the former Communist Party less than 10 per cent of the seats in the new parliament. In Czechoslovakia the communist government of Gustav Husak resisted demands for reform until mass public demonstrations and strikes forced its resignation in December 1989. The well-known writer and human rights activist Vaclav Havel became the new president and head of a coalition government containing a majority of non-communists. The Communist Party proved more skilful in Bulgaria. Political demise was avoided by volunteering the resignation of President Todor Zhivkov in 1989, after 35 years in power, and changing the party's name to the 'Bulgarian Socialist Party'. By contrast, neighbouring Romania experienced violent revolutionary change. The dictatorship of Nicolae Ceauşescu, which had ruled the country since 1965, was overthrown in December 1989. Ceauşescu was captured and executed.

Momentous developments also took place in Germany. The year 1989 marked the fortieth anniversary of the founding of East Germany. Instead of celebrating, however, increasingly large numbers of East Germans showed their discontent with prevailing conditions by escaping to West Germany. Travelling ostensibly as tourists to Hungary, they took advantage of the newly opened border between Hungary and Austria to cross into the West. In East Germany itself, mass public demonstrations demanded political and economic freedom. The communist leader, Erich Honecker, was compelled to resign on 18 October. Amid growing political confusion, the government announced on 9 November that trips abroad including travel to and from West Berlin would be permitted without restrictions. On that night East German guards proceeded to open the Berlin Wall for the first time since 1961. During the following weekend two million East Germans took their chance to visit West Berlin. The opening of the Berlin Wall became an international media event that provided not only East Germans but the world with a vivid and emotive symbol of the collapse of communist authority. Moreover, despite the presence of substantial numbers of Soviet troops in East Germany, no military intervention was forthcoming from the Soviet Union.

Presented with an opportunity to determine their political future, the people of East Germany chose reunification with West Germany. The prospect of a united Germany, however, revived memories of the two world wars and evoked particular anxiety in Poland and the Soviet Union. The West German chancellor, Helmut Kohl, assured Gorbachev, however, that his country recognized the permanence of existing borders with Poland and that Soviet troops could remain in East Germany until 1994. In fact, West Germany agreed to finance the cost of Soviet military withdrawal, amounting to more than $7 billion. 'We cannot forget the past', Gorbachev told Kohl, and he added: 'But we have to look towards Europe and take the road of co-operation with the great German nation' (Gorbachev, 1996, p. 534). With the Soviet leader's acquiescence the drive towards German reunification gathered remarkable speed and was completed on 3 October 1990. The United States, Soviet Union, Britain and France also formally relinquished their occupation rights and thereby ended an arrangement that had initially been regarded as temporary but had lasted for 45 years.

In the West, the political changes in Eastern Europe were observed with a mixture of surprise and confusion. George Bush, who had been elected to the American presidency in 1988, wanted friendly relations with the Soviets and wished to see the successful implementation of reforms throughout the communist bloc. He believed, however, that orderly and peaceful change in Eastern Europe was dependent upon the acquiescence of the Soviet Union and also on Gorbachev remaining in power. In the circumstances, American interference would only be counter-productive. On a visit to Poland and Hungary in July 1989 Bush privately told their leaders: 'We're not here to make you choose between East and West' (Oberdorfer, 1992, p. 355). The cooperative and friendly relationship between the superpowers was exemplified in the summit meeting held on warships off the coast of Malta in December 1989, when Gorbachev remarked that it was no longer Soviet policy to force the United States out of Europe. In what was essentially a renunciation of the doctrine of Marxism-Leninism he added: 'The Soviet Union will never, under any circumstances, start a war with the United States and, what is more, is not prepared to regard it as an enemy' (Gorbachev, 1996, p. 514). Bush expressed similarly friendly views at the closing press conference:

> We stand at the threshold of a brand new era of U.S.–Soviet relations. There is virtually no problem in the world – and certainly no problem in Europe – that improvement in the U.S.–Soviet relationship will not help to ameliorate. A better U.S.–Soviet relationship is to be valued in and of itself, but it also should be an instrument of positive change for the world. (Oberdorfer, 1992, p. 383)

In July 1991 Bush travelled to Moscow to sign the START I treaty, which set reduced limits on the numbers of launchers and nuclear warheads. The treaty was essentially a replacement and substitute for the SALT II agreement, which had never been formally ratified. Gorbachev described his discussions with the American president as reflecting 'a high degree of mutual trust, despite divergent opinions on some issues; and a high degree of agreement not only on current but also on new, emerging problems' (Gorbachev, 1996, p. 618).

Although the concept of partnership with the United States was most gratifying to Gorbachev, his absolute priority since coming to power in 1985 had been to revitalize the Soviet Union. The impact of domestic reforms proved, however, to be limited and extremely disappointing. Quite simply, Gorbachev could not revive a moribund economy that was blighted with chronic mismanagement and inefficiency. Industrial and agricultural production fell below government targets, while inflation, the foreign debt and trade deficits sharply increased. The resulting economic discontent stimulated not only widespread criticism both of *perestroika* and Gorbachev's leadership but also demands from ethnic groups for local autonomy and even independence. The latter development was highly significant because there were more than 100 different nationalities within the Soviet Union. Nationalism was strongest and most readily organized as a political movement in the three Baltic states of Estonia, Latvia and Lithuania. They saw *perestroika* as an opportunity to regain the independence which had been lost in 1940 when the Baltic republics had been forcibly annexed by Stalin. In November 1988 Lithuania declared itself a soveriegn state, an action imitated in 1990 by Estonia and Latvia. Nationalist risings also erupted in other regions, especially in Kazakhstan and Nagorno-Karabakh, where *perestroika* was condemned as unacceptable interference from Moscow with local traditions and political organizations.

In contrast to his non-interventionist policy towards Eastern Europe, Gorbachev was prepared to use armed force to maintain the Union. The most notorious episode occurred at Tbilisi in Georgia in April 1989 when troops killed 19 demonstrators, 16 of whom were women. Similar violence against protesters at Tiananmen Square in Beijing in June 1989 maintained the authority of the Chinese government, but its use in the Soviet Union only served to discredit Gorbachev and contributed to the growing demands for his removal from office. Gorbachev eventually resigned as general secretary in August 1991. By that time the process of internal disintegration had proceeded to such an extent that the Soviet Union no longer existed as a sovereign entity. On 8 December 1991, the Soviet Union came to an end when 11 of the 15 republics reformed themselves as the Commonwealth of Independent States (CIS).

End of the Cold War

Contemporary observers were stunned by the speed and magnitude of the changes taking place in Eastern Europe and the Soviet Union. They found it hard to comprehend that they were actually witnessing a major turning point in twentieth-century history, equivalent to the Bolshevik Revolution in 1917 or the Allied victories over Germany and Japan in 1945. The perplexity prevailing in 1989 was understandable. Although Soviet economic and military prowess had always been clouded in secrecy, it was generally believed in the West that, whatever its deficiencies, the system of a command economy would enable the Soviet Union to maintain the status of superpower for the foreseeable future. Indeed, the Cold War had lasted for such a long time that it was naturally assumed that it must continue for several more decades. There were also too many vested interests at stake. The bipolar conflict appeared to serve the purposes of the two superpowers very well by providing a rationale for them to lead and dominate their respective alliance systems. In material terms, within both the United States and the Soviet Union 'military-industrial complexes' had evolved whose existence and well-being were dependent on the prolongation of international rivalry and competition. Indeed, political leaders on both sides of the Iron Curtain had built their careers around their 'cold warrior' credentials. Despite occasional war scares, however, the relationship between the superpowers stressed 'peaceful coexistence' rather than permanent military confrontation. The periods of 'thaw' in the 1950s and *détente* in the 1970s showed that they were willing to discuss arms control and defuse world tensions, but a negotiated 'ending' of the Cold War had never been given serious consideration.

In 1989, however, the structure of international relations was dramatically transformed not from 'above' but from 'below' by the 'revolutions' in Eastern Europe. The most momentous single event was the opening of the Berlin Wall, which had stood for almost three decades as the prominent and enduring symbol of the Cold War in

Europe. Government officials and politicians in the West looked on in seeming amazement as the people of Eastern Europe spontaneously took the initiative in bringing about the peaceful overthrow of the Iron Curtain. A critical factor in their success was undoubtedly Gorbachev's decision not to resort to military retaliation. The Soviet leader had hoped that *perestroika* would be received positively in the satellite states. However, his celebrated speech at the United Nations in December 1988 had stated that all nations possessed 'freedom of choice' (Gorbachev, 1996, p. 460). The people of Eastern Europe took him at his word and opted for the West as their preferred model of political, economic and moral progress. The events of 1989 were therefore crucially important in delivering a humiliating and shattering blow to the advocates of international communism. The doctrine of Marxism–Leninism was thoroughly discredited because it was the Eastern bloc, not the West, that was in terminal economic decline. The Czech dissident Vaclav Havel likened the revelation to the story by Hans Christian Anderson in which the boy cries that 'the Emperor is naked' and thereby compels everyone to acknowledge a truth that had been denied for so long. Although the communist system would continue to prevail in China and Cuba, the 'ideological' Cold War was resolved to the satisfaction of most of the world in 1989 in favour of the Western values of democracy and free market economics.

The 'loss' of Eastern Europe in 1989–90 significantly reduced the geopolitical influence of the Soviet Union. It was, however, part of a general Soviet retreat from overseas commitments, exemplified in the military withdrawal in Afghanistan and the substantial reduction of financial aid to Cuba. According to Mikhail Gorbachev, the Soviet Union wanted to be a friend and not an enemy of the West. His intentions were translated into deeds as the Soviet Union entered into a number of arms control agreements with the West, most notably the INF treaty in 1987 and the START I treaty in 1991. At the same time provision was made for regular and direct consultation between senior commanders in NATO and the Warsaw Pact countries. At the Paris meeting of the Conference on Security and Cooperation in Europe, delegates from the two military alliances jointly issued a statement that they were 'no longer adversaries' and would 'build new partnerships and extend to each other the hand of friendship' (Garthoff, 1994b, p. 621). The passing of the 'military' Cold War was signified on 21 November 1990, when the CSCE Conference formally proclaimed 'the end of the Cold War'.

Despite the proclamation of the CSCE Conference, it was hard to accept that the Cold War had definitely 'ended' so long as both superpowers maintained massive nuclear arsenals directed mainly at each other. In 1991, however, the Soviet Union collapsed as a nation state. As a result the bipolar system that had dominated international affairs since the end of World War II ceased to exist. But the United States still remained a superpower. In place of the former Soviet Union, however, was a new nation known as the Commonwealth of Independent States, which was so troubled by grave economic and political difficulties that it could hardly be regarded as a superpower. The CIS possessed large conventional and nuclear forces, but its military capabilities were severely undermined by internal demoralization and the defection of the Eastern European states from the Warsaw Pact. In the opinion of the chairman of the American Joint Chiefs of Staff, the Warsaw Pact was 'a shambles' (Powell, 1995, p. 453). It was formally dissolved in 1991. By contrast, the Atlantic Alliance, in the form of NATO, remained intact and had actually been strengthened by the inclusion of the new, reunified Germany.

When the political disintegration of the Soviet Union became a reality, a mood of triumphalism seized the West. Cold War politics had traditionally been regarded as a zero-sum game in which a gain for one side was by definition a loss for the other. The collapse of the communist system was naturally interpreted, therefore, as a victory for the West over the East. Personal credit was fastened on the United States and especially on Ronald Reagan, who was acclaimed as 'the man who ended the Cold War' (Meese, 1992, p. 163). Under Reagan's leadership the United States had recaptured the sense of national self-confidence and purpose that had been severely undermined during the harrowing years of Vietnam and Watergate. He had also been instrumental in achieving a substantial military build-up that, his admirers argued, had scared the Soviets into offering concessions on strategic arms control and withdrawing from Third World adventurism. Secretary of State George Shultz considered that Reagan's strategy of 'negotiation from strength' had produced a 'turning point' in modern history. He explained: 'When our country's military strength was built up to a point where our Soviet rivals recognized that they could not match us, when they perceived that we might actually use our strength to repel aggression, and as their own system indisputably failed the Soviet people even as it abused them – then came the turning point' (Shultz, 1993, p. 1131).

To what extent Reagan caused or simply accelerated the demise of the Soviet Union is a matter of debate. During the 1980s the Soviets certainly fell behind the United States in terms of actual military and economic power. Nevertheless, the Soviet Union remained a formidable nuclear power and, despite its many shortcomings, the Soviet economy still continued to function. In fact, with the rise to power of Mikhail Gorbachev in 1985 a Soviet leader once again assumed a prominent role in world affairs reminiscent of Khrushchev's during the 1950s. Gorbachev's boldness of vision and action provided the catalyst for a series of momentous changes which dramatically challenged and confounded diplomatic attitudes that had become fixed and entrenched. In order to achieve internal reforms, the new Soviet leader wanted to end the confrontational relationship between East and West. This resulted in sweeping proposals to abolish nuclear weapons, the renunciation of the Brezhnev Doctrine, and the statement that the United States was no longer an enemy of the Soviet Union. In effect, Gorbachev unilaterally declared a peaceful end to the Cold War.

Despite his undoubted ability and personal magnetism, Gorbachev was as much the prisoner as the master of events. 'Gorbachev knew what his problems were but he acted both too fast and too slowly: too fast for the tolerance of his system, and too slowly to arrest the accelerating collapse', remarked Henry Kissinger (Kissinger, 1994, p. 799). The Soviet leader was ambitious and charming, but he was also impatient and abrasive. He sought to impose *perestroika* on the Soviet people and was insensitive to ethnic issues. Critics of Gorbachev's foreign policy argued that he was motivated more by weakness than by strength of purpose. For example, the decision to pull Soviet troops out of Afghanistan was interpreted as a belated recognition that, after almost a decade, the war of attrition had been lost. The rejection of military intervention in Eastern Europe similarly reflected not far-sighted statesmanship but the inherent confusion of Gorbachev's diplomacy. Retaliation to suppress political reforms would not only contradict the implementation of *perestroika* in the Soviet Union but also upset the attempt to seek a new, cooperative relationship with the West and NATO. The image was of an increasingly forlorn Gorbachev presiding over a nation that was falling apart.

Even though the history of the Cold War has revolved around the activities of notable leaders, ranging from Churchill, Roosevelt and Stalin in the 1940s to Nixon and Brezhnev in the 1970s, it is too simplistic to attribute the ending of the Cold War solely to the merits or deficiencies of two individuals – Reagan and Gorbachev. In fact, their policies were not as 'new' as they maintained. The military build-up associated with Reagan actually began during the Carter administration in 1979. Gorbachev's *perestroika* was, strictly speaking, a continuation of the policy of 'acceleration' introduced by Yury Andropov. Delving farther into the past, it could be argued that Reagan was following the policy of rearmament outlined more than three decades earlier in NSC-68 or that Gorbachev was imitating the diplomatic initiative proposed by Malenkov after Stalin's death in 1953. Indeed, on the American side, the strategy of 'containment', as conceived by George Kennan in 1947, had always been regarded as a 'long-term' effort. According to Henry Kissinger, the ending of the Cold War was 'a result of the confluence of forty years of American bipartisan effort and seventy years of communist ossification' (Kissinger, 1994, p. 802).

Kissinger was convinced that the United States had 'won' the Cold War. If so, it could not be considered a total victory. Unlike the situation after World War II, there was no great military triumph to proclaim in 1991. In fact, when compared with 1945, the United States in 1991 was neither so optimistic about the future nor in possession of such a commanding lead in military and economic power over other nations. Of the former wartime allies, the Soviet Union had disintegrated while Britain had declined to the status of a middle-ranking world power. The most remarkable rise, especially in economic terms, had been that of the enemy nations, Germany and Japan. Indeed, it might be argued that they had emerged as the real beneficiaries or even 'winners' of the Cold War. Such an interpretation, however, distorts the achievement of American foreign policy, which had set out in the late 1940s to protect and promote the political and economic recovery of Western Europe. In the process, the prediction of Marxism-Leninism that capitalism would inevitably decline and communism would prevail was proved wrong. This only became evident during the 1980s, when Reagan led a resurgence of American power that coincided with turmoil in the Soviet economy and political system arising from reforms introduced by Gorbachev. 'At the present moment in world history,' Harry Truman had stated in March 1947, 'nearly every nation must choose between alternative ways of life.' He had lamented, however, that 'the choice is too often not a free one' (Halle, 1967, p. 120). But a 'free' choice suddenly materialized in 1989 and the people of Eastern Europe unequivocally chose the Western 'way of life'. After more than four decades the policy of containment was finally vindicated. Under the leadership of the United States, the West had defeated the Soviet Union and 'won' the Cold War.

Guide to Further Reading

The most useful documentary collection for this study has been Arthur M. Schlesinger Jr. (ed.), *The dynamics of world power: a documentary history of United States foreign policy, 1945–1973*. The five volumes stress American policy, but cover the whole world and include the period up to 1973. Informative textbooks outlining the historical background to the Cold War are Christopher J. Bartlett, *The global conflict*, and William R. Keylor, *The twentieth century world*. Henry Kissinger, *Diplomacy*, is an impressive and articulate overview which concentrates on the twentieth century. For basic factual information on political events see Peter Calvocoressi, *World politics since 1945*. Specific studies covering the whole period of the Cold War from 1945 to 1991 are only just beginning to be published. Ralph Levering, *The Cold War: a post-Cold War history*, is thoughtful and interpretative, J.P. Dunbabin, *The Cold War*, is detailed and well-informed, while Richard Crockatt, *The fifty years war*, offers a reflective 'systems' approach. John Young, *Cold War Europe, 1945–1989*, is a straightforward and factual study of European developments. The relationship between the two superpowers is competently analysed in Peter Boyle, *American–Soviet relations*. The same subject is also explored in the textbook by Walter LaFeber, *America, Russia and the Cold War*, and in the perceptive articles contained in Thomas G. Paterson, *Meeting the communist threat*. For an outstanding study of American 'strategy' throughout the Cold War see John L. Gaddis, *Strategies of containment*.

On the origins of the Cold War, Thomas G. Paterson and Robert J. McMahon (eds), *The origins of the Cold War*, and Melvyn P. Leffler and David S. Painter (eds), *Origins of the Cold War*, are excellent collections of readings which make accessible the wide range of historical interpretations on this subject. Martin McCauley, *The origins of the Cold War, 1941–1949*, and Michael Dockrill, *The Cold War, 1945-1963*, provide concise and readable overviews. For a sampling of more specialist studies see Herbert

Feis, *From trust to terror*, for the 'orthodox' view, Joyce and Gabriel Kolko, *The limits of power*, for a 'revisionist' approach, and John L. Gaddis, *The United States and the origins of the Cold War*, for a 'post-revisionist' analysis.

The foreign policies of the Roosevelt and Truman administrations are examined at considerable length in Robert Dallek, *Franklin D. Roosevelt and American foreign policy*, and Melvyn P. Leffler, *A preponderance of power*. Charles L. Mee, *Meeting at Potsdam*, serves as a very readable introduction to the machinations of the Big Three. Two important memoirs that give a personal insight into diplomatic attitudes and the making of American foreign policy during the late 1940s are George F. Kennan, *Memoirs, 1925–1950*, and Dean Acheson, *Present at the creation*. For the Soviet perspective see William Taubman, *Stalin's American policy*, and Caroline Kennedy-Pipe, *Stalin's Cold War*. Milovan Djilas, *Conversations with Stalin*, reveals the menacing atmosphere of the Kremlin.

Reliable and informative guides to the causes and course of the Korean War are Peter Lowe, *The origins of the Korean War*, and Burton I. Kaufman, *The Korean War*. Stephen E. Ambrose, *Eisenhower: the president*, is a readable survey of the presidential years, while Robert A. Divine, *Eisenhower and the Cold War*, offers a concise analysis of Eisenhower's foreign policy. For important articles discussing the significance of John Foster Dulles see Richard H. Immerman (ed.), *John Foster Dulles and the diplomacy of the Cold War*. The excitement of the Kennedy presidency is evoked in Arthur M. Schlesinger Jr., *A thousand days*. Michael R. Beschloss, *The crisis years: Kennedy and Khrushchev, 1960–1963*, gives a virtually blow-by-blow account of the stormy diplomatic relationship between the two leaders, while Thomas G. Paterson (ed.), *Kennedy's quest for victory*, provides analytical articles that critically assess Kennedy's diplomatic aims and achievements. Robert E. Quirk, *Fidel Castro*, is a large biographical study of the Cuban leader and is highly informative on relations between the United States and Cuba. On the Cuban Missile Crisis, Robert A. Divine (ed.), *The Cuban Missile Crisis*, provides a very useful collection of readings. Robert F. Kennedy, *Thirteen days*, gives the account of a prominent insider, while Raymond L. Garthoff, *Reflections on the Cuban Missile Crisis*, offers a scholarly perspective of events.

Lyndon B. Johnson, *The vantage point*, is a self-serving memoir, but it is revealing about his attitude towards foreign affairs. Johnson's diplomacy is subject to scholarly examination in Warren I. Cohen and Nancy Bernkopf Tucker (eds), *Lyndon Johnson confronts the world*. Of the many books on Vietnam, Stanley Karnow, *Vietnam*, gives an excellent overview of the country and its history, George C. Herring, *America's longest war*, is a readable and perceptive study of America's involvement in the war, and George D. Moss, *Vietnam: an American ordeal*, provides a useful and informative survey. The disillusioning experience of American soldiers who served in Vietnam is memorably expressed in Neil Sheehan, *A bright shining lie*.

Although it is more than 1,000 pages in length Raymond L. Garthoff, *Detente and confrontation*, is indispensable reading for an understanding of superpower relations during the 1970s. For a shorter and more specific analysis of American foreign policy from Nixon to Bush see Richard Melanson, *Reconstructing consensus*. The habit of American presidents and their national security advisers rushing into print has provided copious material for studying the decade of the 1970s. Richard Nixon, *The memoirs of Richard Nixon*, and Henry Kissinger, *The White House years* and *Years of upheaval*, explain events from the perspective of the White House. For similar works covering the Carter administration see Jimmy Carter, *Keeping faith*, and Zbigniew Brzezinski, *Power and principle*. Seymour M. Hersh, *Kissinger*, is severely critical of Kissinger's foreign policy, while Walter Isaacson, *Kissinger*, offers a more balanced appraisal. For Brezhnev's foreign policy see Robin Edmonds, *Soviet foreign policy*. The significance of the deterioration of superpower relations arising from the invasion of Afghanistan in 1979 is the theme of Fred Halliday, *The making of the second Cold War*.

Diplomatic events during the 1980s are examined in great detail by Raymond L. Garthoff, *The great transition*. An even longer work extending to more than 1,000 pages is George P. Shultz, *Turmoil and triumph*, which gives chapter and verse on what Shultz regards as the momentous achievements of the Reagan presidency. A contrasting perspective is presented in Mikhail Gorbachev, *Memoirs*. For a scholarly assessment of the Soviet leader see Archie Brown, *The Gorbachev factor*. The winding down of the Cold War is fully reported in the extremely well-informed journalistic accounts of Don Oberdorfer, *The turn*, and Michael R. Beschloss and Strobe Talbott, *At the highest levels*. The critical significance of the 1989 revolutions in Eastern Europe is highlighted in Gale Stokes, *The walls came tumbling down*. Despite being an exercise in 'instant historical analysis,' Michael Hogan (ed.), *The end of the Cold War*, presents concise essays on the end of the Cold War written by distinguished scholars representing a wide spectrum of historical ideas and national backgrounds.

Bibliography

Acheson, Dean 1970: *Present at the creation: my years in the state department*. London: Hamish Hamilton.

Achilles, Theodore C. 1985: The Omaha milkman. In André de Staercke (ed.) *NATO's anxious birth*. London: Hurst.

Alperovitz, Gar 1965: *Atomic diplomacy: Hiroshima and Potsdam*. New York: Simon and Schuster.

Ambrose, Stephen E. 1983a: *Rise to globalism: American foreign policy since 1938*. London: Penguin.

Ambrose, Stephen E. 1983b: *Eisenhower: the soldier*. New York: Simon and Schuster.

Ambrose, Stephen E. 1984: *Eisenhower: the president*. London: Allen and Unwin.

Anderson, Terry H. 1981: *The United States, Great Britain and the Cold War, 1944–1947*. Columbia: University of Missouri Press.

Bartlett, Christopher J. 1994: *The global conflict: the international rivalry of the great powers, 1880–1990*. London: Longman.

Baylis, John 1990: Britain and the formation of NATO. In Joseph Smith (ed.) *The origins of NATO*. Exeter: Exeter University Press.

Bernstein, Barton J. (ed.) 1970: *Politics and policies of the Truman administration*. Chicago: Quadrangle.

Beschloss, Michael R. 1991: *The crisis years: Kennedy and Khrushchev, 1960–1963*. New York: HarperCollins.

Beschloss, Michael R. and Talbott, Strobe 1993: *At the highest levels: the inside story of the end of the Cold War*. Boston: Little, Brown.

Boyle, Peter G. 1993: *American–Soviet relations: from the Russian revolution to the fall of communism*. London: Routledge.

Brown, Archie 1996: *The Gorbachev factor*. Oxford: Oxford University Press.

Brzezinski, Zbigniew 1983: *Power and principle: memoirs of the national security adviser, 1977–1981*. New York: Farrar, Straus and Giroux.

Calvocoressi, Peter 1982: *World politics since 1945*. London: Longman.

Carter, Jimmy 1995: *Keeping faith: memoirs of a president*. Fayetteville: University of Arkansas Press.

Clay, Lucius D. 1950: *Decision in Germany*. New York: Doubleday.

Clifford, Clark 1991: *Counsel to the president*. New York: Random House.

Cohen, Warren I. and Tucker, Nancy Bernkopf (eds) 1994: *Lyndon Johnson confronts the world: American foreign policy, 1963–1968*. Cambridge: Cambridge University Press.

Cook, Don 1989: *Forging the alliance: NATO, 1945–1950*. London: Secker and Warburg.

Crockatt, Richard 1995: *The fifty years war: the United States and the Soviet Union in world politics, 1941–1991*. London: Routledge.

Dallek, Robert 1979: *Franklin D. Roosevelt and American foreign policy, 1932–1945*. New York: Oxford University Press.

Dallin, Alexander 1962: *The Soviet Union at the United Nations: an inquiry into Soviet motives and objectives*. London: Methuen.

Delmas, Claude 1985: A change of heart. In André de Staercke (ed.) *NATO's anxious birth*. London: Hurst.

Divine, Robert A. 1981: *Eisenhower and the Cold War*. New York: Oxford University Press.

Divine, Robert A. (ed.) 1988: *The Cuban Missile Crisis*. New York: Markus Wiener.

Djilas, Milovan 1962: *Conversations with Stalin*. London: Penguin.

Dockrill, Michael 1988: *The Cold War, 1945–1963*. London: Macmillan.

Dunbabin, J. P. 1994: *The Cold War: the great powers and their allies*. London: Longman.

Edmonds, Robin 1983: *Soviet foreign policy: the Brezhnev years*. Oxford: Oxford University Press.

Feis, Herbert 1970: *From trust to terror: the onset of the Cold War, 1945–1950*. New York: Norton.

Fleming, Denna F. 1961: *The Cold War and its origins, 1917–1960*. 2 vols. New York: Doubleday.

Ford, Gerald R. 1979: *A time to heal: the autobiography of Gerald R. Ford*. London: W.H. Allen.

Frazier, Robert 1984: Did Britain start the Cold War? *Historical journal*, 27, 715–27.

Gaddis, John L. 1972: *The United States and the origins of the Cold War, 1941-1947*. New York: Columbia University Press.

Gaddis, John L. 1982: *Strategies of containment: a critical appraisal of postwar American national security policy*. Oxford: Oxford University Press.

Gaddis, John L. 1983: The emerging post-revisionist synthesis on the origins of the Cold War. *Diplomatic history*, 7, 171–204.

Gaddis, John L. 1974: Was the Truman Doctrine a real turning point? *Foreign Affairs*, 52, 386–402.

Garthoff, Raymond L. 1989: *Reflections on the Cuban Missile Crisis.* Washington DC: Brookings Institution.

Garthoff, Raymond L. 1994a: *Detente and confrontation: American–Soviet relations from Nixon to Reagan.* Washington DC: Brookings Institution.

Garthoff, Raymond L. 1994b: *The great transition: American–Soviet relations and the end of the Cold War.* Washington DC: Brookings Institution.

Goncharov, Serge N., Lewis, John W. and Xue Litai 1993: *Uncertain partners: Stalin, Mao, and the Korean War.* Stanford: Stanford University Press.

Gorbachev, Mikhail 1996: *Memoirs.* London: Doubleday.

Graebner, Norman A. 1984: *America as a world power: a realist appraisal from Wilson to Reagan.* Wilmington: Scholarly Resources.

Haig, Alexander M., Jr. 1984: *Caveat: realism, Reagan, and foreign policy.* London: Weidenfeld and Nicolson.

Halle, Louis J. 1967: *The Cold War as history.* London: Chatto and Windus.

Halliday, Fred 1986: *The making of the second Cold War.* London: Verso.

Hathaway, Robert M. 1981: *Ambiguous partnership: Britain and America, 1944–1947.* New York: Columbia University Press.

Herring, George C. 1979: *America's longest war: the United States and Vietnam, 1950–1975.* New York: Knopf.

Hersh, Seymour M. 1983: *Kissinger: the price of power.* London: Faber and Faber.

Hogan, Michael J. 1987: *The Marshall plan: America, Britain and the reconstruction of Western Europe, 1947–1952.* Cambridge: Cambridge University Press.

Hogan, Michael J. (ed.) 1992: *The end of the Cold War: its meaning and implications.* Cambridge: Cambridge University Press.

Horowitz, David 1965: *The free world colossus: a critique of American foreign policy in the Cold War.* New York: Hill and Wang.

Immerman, Richard H. (ed.) 1990: *John Foster Dulles and the diplomacy of the Cold War.* Princeton NJ: Princeton University Press.

Isaacson, Walter 1992: *Kissinger: a biography.* New York: Simon and Schuster.

Johnson, Lyndon B. 1972: *The vantage point: perspectives on the presidency, 1963–1969.* London: Weidenfeld and Nicolson.

Karnow, Stanley 1984: *Vietnam: a history.* London: Penguin.

Kaufman, Burton I. 1986: *The Korean War: challenges in crisis, credibility, and command.* New York: Knopf.

Kennan, George F. 1968: *Memoirs, 1925–1950.* London: Hutchinson.

Kennedy, Robert F. 1969: *Thirteen days: a memoir of the Cuban Missile Crisis*. New York: Norton.

Kennedy-Pipe, Caroline 1995: *Stalin's Cold War: Soviet strategies in Europe, 1943 to 1956*. Manchester: Manchester University Press.

Keylor, William R. 1992: *The twentieth century world: an international history*. New York: Oxford University Press.

Kissinger, Henry 1979: *The White House years*. London: Weidenfeld and Nicolson.

Kissinger, Henry 1982: *Years of upheaval*. London: Weidenfeld and Nicolson.

Kissinger, Henry 1994: *Diplomacy*. New York: Simon and Schuster.

Kolko, Gabriel 1968: *The politics of war: the world and United States foreign policy, 1943–1945*. London: Weidenfeld and Nicolson.

Kolko, Joyce and Kolko, Gabriel 1972: *The limits of power: the world and United States foreign policy, 1945–1954*. London: Harper and Row.

Krock, Arthur 1968: *Memoirs: sixty years on the firing line*. New York: Funk and Wagnalls.

Kuklick, Bruce 1972: *American policy and the division of Germany: the clash with Russia over reparations*. Ithaca NY: Cornell University Press.

Kuniholm, Bruce R. 1980: *The origins of the Cold War in the Near East: great power conflict and diplomacy in Iran, Turkey and Greece*. Princeton NJ: Princeton University Press.

LaFeber, Walter 1976: *America, Russia and the Cold War, 1945–1975*. New York: Wiley.

Lebow, Richard Ned and Stein, Janice Gross 1994: *We all lost the Cold War*. Princeton NJ: Princeton University Press.

Leffler, Melvyn P. 1984: The American conception of national security and the beginnings of the Cold War, 1945–1948. *American historical review*, 89, 346–400.

Leffler, Melvyn P. 1992: *A preponderance of power: national security, the Truman administration and the Cold War*. Stanford: Stanford University Press.

Leffler, Melvyn P. 1994: *The specter of communism: the United States and the origins of the Cold War, 1917–1953*. New York: Hill and Wang.

Leffler, Melvyn P. and Painter, David S. (eds) 1994: *Origins of the Cold War: an international history*. London: Routledge.

Levering, Ralph B. 1994: *The Cold War: a post-Cold War history*. Arlington Heights: Harlan Davidson.

Lowe, Peter 1986: *The origins of the Korean War*. London: Longman.

Lundestad, Geir 1990: *The American 'empire' and other studies of US foreign policy in a comparative perspective*. Oxford: Oxford University Press.

Lyons, Terence 1994: Keeping Africa off the agenda. In Warren I. Cohen and Nancy Bernkopf Tucker (eds) *Lyndon Johnson confronts the world: American foreign policy, 1963–1968*. Cambridge: Cambridge University Press.

McCauley, Martin 1995: *The origins of the Cold War, 1941–1949*. London: Longman.

Maddox Robert J. 1973: *The new left and the origins of the Cold War*. Princeton NJ: Princeton University Press.

Manchester, William 1979: *American caesar: Douglas MacArthur, 1880–1964*. London: Hutchinson.

May, Ernest R. 1973: *'Lessons' of the past*. New York: Oxford University Press.

Mee, Charles L. 1975: *Meeting at Potsdam*. New York: Evans.

Meese, Edwin 1992: *With Reagan: the inside story*. Washington DC: Regnery Gateway.

Melanson, Richard A. 1991: *Reconstructing consensus: American foreign policy since the Vietnam War*. New York: St Martin's Press.

Millis Walter (ed.) 1951: *The Forrestal diaries*. New York: Viking.

Moss, George D. 1990: *Vietnam: an American ordeal*. Englewood Cliffs NJ: Prentice Hall.

New York Times 1971: *The Pentagon papers*. London: Routledge and Kegan Paul.

Nixon, Richard 1978: *The memoirs of Richard Nixon*. London: Sidgwick and Jackson.

Oberdorfer, Don 1992: *The turn: how the Cold War came to an end*. London: Jonathan Cape.

Osgood, Robert E. 1962: *Nato: the entangling alliance*. Chicago: University of Chicago Press.

Paterson, Thomas G. 1979: *On every front: the making of the Cold War*. New York: Norton.

Paterson, Thomas G. 1988: *Meeting the communist threat: Truman to Reagan*. New York: Oxford University Press.

Paterson, Thomas G. (ed.) 1989: *Kennedy's quest for victory: American foreign policy, 1961–1963*. New York: Oxford University Press.

Paterson, Thomas G. and McMahon, Robert J. (eds) 1991: *The origins of the Cold War*. Lexington: D. C. Heath.

Paterson, Thomas G., Clifford, J. Garry and Hagan, Kenneth J. 1995: *American foreign relations: a history since 1895*. Vol. 2. Lexington: D. C. Heath.

Ponomaryov, B. (ed.) 1974: *History of Soviet foreign policy, 1945–1970*. Moscow: Progress Publishers.

Powell, Colin L. 1995: *A soldier's way: an autobiography*. London: Hutchinson.

Quirk, Robert E. 1993: *Fidel Castro*. New York: Norton.

Reagan, Ronald 1990: *An American life: the autobiography*. New York: Simon and Schuster.

Salinger, Pierre 1967: *With Kennedy*. London: Jonathan Cape.

Schlesinger, Arthur M., Jr. 1965: *A thousand days: John F. Kennedy in the White House*. London: André Deutsch.

Schlesinger, Arthur M., Jr. 1967: Origins of the Cold War. *Foreign affairs*, 46, 22–52.

Schlesinger, Arthur M., Jr. (ed.) 1983: *The dynamics of world power: a documentary history of United States foreign policy, 1945–1973*. 5 vols. New York: Chelsea House.

Sheehan, Neil 1988: *A bright shining lie: John Paul Vann and America in Vietnam*. New York: Random House.

Sherwin, Martin 1975: *A world destroyed: the atomic bomb and the grand alliance*. New York: Knopf.

Shultz, George P. 1993: *Turmoil and triumph: diplomacy, power, and the victory of the American ideal*. New York: Charles Scribner's Sons.

Siracusa, Joseph M. (ed.) 1978: *The American diplomatic revolution: a documentary history of the Cold War, 1941–1947*. Milton Keynes: Open University Press.

Spanier, John W. 1960: *American foreign policy since World War II*. New York: Praeger.

Stokes, Gale 1993: *The walls came tumbling down: the collapse of communism in Eastern Europe*. New York: Oxford University Press.

Talbott, Strobe 1979: *Endgame: the inside story of SALT II*. New York: Harper and Row.

Talbott, Strobe 1989: *The master of the game: Paul Nitze and the nuclear peace*. New York: Vintage Books.

Taubman, William 1982: *Stalin's American policy: from entente to detente to Cold War*. New York: Columbia University Press.

Thomas, Hugh 1986: *Armed truce: the beginnings of the Cold War, 1945–46*. London: Hamish Hamilton.

Thorne, Christopher 1978: *Allies of a kind: the United States, Britain, and the war against Japan*. Oxford: Oxford University Press.

Truman, Harry S. 1955: *Memoirs: Year of decisions 1945*. London: Hodder and Stoughton.

Truman, Harry S. 1956: *Memoirs: Years of trial and hope 1946–1953*. London: Hodder and Stoughton.

Ulam, Adam B. 1973: *The rivals: America and Russia since World War II*. London: Allen Lane.

Walton, Richard J. 1973: *Cold War and counter-revolution: the foreign policy of John F. Kennedy*. Baltimore: Penguin.

Williams, William A. 1962: *The tragedy of American diplomacy*. New York: Dell.

Yergin, Daniel 1978: *Shattered peace: the origins of the Cold War and the national security state.* London: André Deutsch.

Young, John W. 1991: *Cold War Europe, 1945–1989: a political history.* London: Edward Arnold.

Abbreviations

ABM	Anti-ballistic missile
ALCM	Air-launched cruise missile
ARVN	Army of the Republic of Vietnam (South Vietnam)
ATB	Advanced Technology Bomber
CENTO	Central Treaty Organization
CFE	Conventional Armed Forces in Europe
CIA	Central Intelligence Agency
CIS	Commonwealth of Independent States
CMEA	Council for Mutual Economic Assistance (Comecon)
Cominform	Communist Information Bureau
Contra	Counter-revolutionary (in Nicaragua)
CSCE	Conference on Security and Cooperation in Europe
DRV	Democratic Republic of Vietnam (North Vietnam)
ECSC	European Coal and Steel Community
EDC	European Defence Community
EEC	European Economic Community
ERP	European Recovery Programme (Marshall Plan)
ERW	Enhanced Radiation Weapon
FNLA	National Front for the Liberation of Angola
FRG	Federal Republic of Germany (West Germany)
FSLN	Sandinista National Liberation Front (in Nicaragua)
GDR	German Democratic Republic (East Germany)
GLCM	Ground-launched cruise missile
IBRD	International Bank for Reconstruction and Development (World Bank)
ICBM	Intercontinental ballistic missile
IMF	International Monetary Fund
INF	Intermediate-range nuclear forces
MAD	Mutual assured destruction

MBFR	Mutual and Balanced Force Reductions
MFN	Most-favoured-nation
MIRV	Multiple independently targeted re-entry vehicle
MPLA	Popular Movement for the Liberation of Angola
MX	Missile Experimental
NATO	North Atlantic Treaty Organization
NLF	National Liberation Front (in South Vietnam)
NSC	National Security Council
OAS	Organization of American States
OAU	Organization of African Unity
OPEC	Organization of Petroleum Exporting Countries
PLO	Palestine Liberation Organization
PRC	People's Republic of China (Red China)
RDF	Rapid Deployment Force
ROK	Republic of Korea (South Korea)
RVN	Republic of Vietnam (South Vietnam)
SAC	Strategic Air Command
SACEUR	Supreme Allied Commander Europe (NATO)
SALT	Strategic Arms Limitation Talks/Treaty
SAM	Surface-to-air missile
SDI	Strategic Defense Initiative
SEATO	South East Asia Treaty Organization
SLBM	Submarine-launched ballistic missile
SRVN	Socialist Republic of Vietnam
SS	Surface-to-surface
START	Strategic Arms Reduction Talks/Treaty
UN	United Nations
UNITA	National Union for the Total Independence of Angola
UNRRA	United Nations Relief and Rehabilitation Administration
US/USA	United States of America
USSR	Union of Soviet Socialist Republics
VC	Vietcong
WEU	Western European Union
WTO	Warsaw Treaty Organization or Warsaw Pact

Index